MACAU AND THE

MACAU AND THE
CASINO COMPLEX

EDITED BY STEFAN AL

CONTRIBUTING EDITORS
KAH-WEE LEE AND NATALIA ECHEVERRI

UNIVERSITY OF NEVADA PRESS | *Reno & Las Vegas*

THE GAMBLING STUDIES SERIES

Series Editor: David G. Schwartz (UNLV)

The Gambling series seeks to cultivate and encourage scholarly investigation of gambling across several disciplines, including history, sociology, economics, psychology, business, and political science. Gambling is both a growing global industry and a widespread pastime throughout the world. The ways that gamblers, governments, and businesses approach gambling are many and varied, and they are a treasure trove of source material for scholars in a variety of disciplines. The series encompasses all forms of gambling, including casinos, lotteries, racing, and sports betting, and will examine organizations owned by private companies, state and national governments, and tribal governments.

Gambling is always in the news—both in Nevada and throughout the world. At present, the major axes of study are problem gambling and the business of gambling. But as gambling continues to grow and become normalized, there will be an increased demand for scholarly work on normative gambling. This series fits that need by publishing books that continue the discourse on problem gambling and those that push the boundaries of what has traditionally need published.

Hand I Played: A Poker Memoir · David Spanier

Futures At Stake: Youth, Gambling, and Society · Howard J. Shaffer, Matthew N. Hall, & Joni Vander Bilt

Dummy Up and Deal: Inside the Culture Of Casino Dealing · H. Lee Barnes

Cutting the Wire: Gaming Prohibition and the Internet · David G. Schwartz

License To Steal: Nevada's Gaming Control System in the Megaresort Age · Jeff Burbank

Casino Accounting and Financial Management · E. Malcolm Greenlees

Rise of the Biggest Little City: An Encyclopedic History of Reno Gaming, 1931-1981 · Dwayne Kling

Gambling, Space, and Time: Shifting Boundaries and Cultures · Pauliina Raento & David G. Schwartz

New Politics of Indian Gaming: The Rise of Reservation Interest Groups · Kenneth N. Hansen & Tracy A. Skopek

All In: The Spread of Gambling in Twentieth-Century United States · Jonathan D. Cohen & David G. Schwartz

University of Nevada Press | Reno, Nevada 89557 USA
www.unpress.nevada.edu
Copyright © 2018 by University of Nevada Press
All rights reserved

LIBRARY OF CONGRESS CATALOGING-IN-PUBLICATION DATA
Names: Al, Stefan, editor. | Lee, Kah Wee. | Echeverri, Natalia.
Title: Macau and the casino complex / [edited] by Stefan Al.
Description: Reno : University of Nevada Press, 2018. | Includes bibliographical references and index. |
    Description based on print version record and CIP data provided by publisher; resource not viewed.
Identifiers: LCCN 2017012561 (print) | LCCN 2017018490 (e-book)
    ISBN 978-1-943859-38-2 (pbk. : alk. paper) | ISBN 978-0-87417-708-4 (e-book)
Subjects: LCSH: Casinos—China—Macau. | Gambling industry—China—Macau. |
    Architecture and society—China—Macau. | Urbanization—China—Macau.
Classification: LCC NA6810 (e-book) | LCC NA6810 .M33 2018 (print) | DDC 725/.76095126—dc23
LC record available at https://lccn.loc.gov/2017012561

The paper used in this book meets the requirements of American National Standard for Information Sciences—Permanence of Paper for Printed Library Materials, ANSI/NISO Z39.48-1992 (R2002).

FIRST PRINTING

Manufactured in the United States of America.

CONTENTS

ACKNOWLEDGMENTS

I thank publisher Justin Race and series
editor David G. Schwartz for their support,
and production manager Virginia Fontana for
her thorough efforts. I am greatly indebted
to contributing editors Kah-Wee Lee and
Natalia Echeverri, who helped shaped this
book in innumerable ways. I am appreciative
of Anthony Lam for his creative design and
Ramune Bartuskaite for her graphic work. I thank
Michael Duckworth for his publishing guidance
and David Brownlee and Thomas Daniell for
their expertise in deciphering architecture.
Hong Kong graduate students in urban design
contributed the vivid drawings, in particular
Alice Weng Sam Iu, Yizhou Feng, and especially
Jun Chen. Finally, I thank the gaming industry
for allowing documentation of casino interiors.

— Stefan Al

MACAU AND THE CASINO COMPLEX

INTRODUCTION

MACAU AND THE CASINO COMPLEX

STEFAN AL

In 2002, the Chinese government, having recently regained Macau after more than a hundred years, ended the monopoly on gambling. Within only five years, this little backwater dethroned Las Vegas to become the world's casino capital. In 2013, Macau took in $45 billion—seven times the gaming revenue of Las Vegas. Today, the Asian city's earnings are more in line with the entire gaming revenue of North America.

It was bound to happen. When Macau, a former Portuguese colony, became a Special Administrative Region within the People's Republic of China in 1999, it was the only place in China where gambling was legal. The Chinese government had already invited foreign companies in to spur innovation in almost every other industry. Only gambling—until then solely controlled by Hong Kong business magnate Stanley Ho—was left.

Given a base of 1.3 billion mainland Chinese formerly denied casino gambling, plus the world's largest growing consumer class, international corporations rushed to the opportunity. In 2003, the government eased visa restrictions to facilitate visits by mainland Chinese to supply the new casinos with customers. Just over a decade later, the top eight of the world's ten highest-grossing casinos were in Macau.

But the profitable liberalization of Macau's gambling industry came with strings attached. The casino influx has permanently transformed the Macau peninsula: seabed has been reclaimed, hillsides have been excavated, roads have become congested, air polluted, and glimmering hotel towers pierce the skyline, dwarfing the nineteenth-century church steeples.

The blueprint for Macau's facelift can be found on the other side of the globe, Las Vegas. Until the five foreign developers came in, three of them from Las Vegas (Las Vegas Sands, Wynn Resorts, and MGM Mirage), Macau's casinos, while garish and neon-bright, were relatively small. The architecture was mostly a mishmash of colonial Portuguese and modernist styles with Chinese elements, such as in the Lisboa casino, a circular, pastel-orange building with ornate white moldings and topped by a conical shape reminiscent of a pagoda. Many of the casinos lacked accommodation and entertainment facilities, since they were meant for gambling only. Gamblers used outside hospitality and entertainment facilities, which were small-to-medium-sized businesses all over Macau that included hotels and saunas.

But the American operators knew profits would increase if gamblers stayed longer on the compound. Back in the 1940s, they pioneered integration of Vegas gambling dens with resort offerings complete with hotels, theaters, and swimming pools in order to create captive audiences willing to stay multiple nights.[1] Now they exported this innovation to Asia.

The first wave of foreign hotel-casinos settled in NAPE (Novos Aterros do Porto Exterior), a newly reclaimed area on the south side of the peninsula. Unlike the irregular and piecemeal downtown, this area was laid out as a grid and was originally intended for offices, apartments, and public parks for locals—until the casinos rolled in.

First came the Sands, a huge, gilded casino with a vast "stadium-style" interior. More global chains followed, including the Wynn and the MGM, which brought to Macau newer architectural styles and plusher interiors. They also added more extravagant attractions, including fountains dancing to Broadway show tunes and a replica of a Portuguese plaza, complete with a copy of Lisbon's train station. Stanley Ho then retaliated with a modern casino-hotel of his own, the Grand Lisboa: a Brazilian-carnival-headdress-inspired, gold skyscraper shaped liked a pineapple, soaring over Macau's skyline.

Nevertheless, the new casino-hotels were still too small. Even though the Wynn complex absorbed six entire city blocks, with two towers housing hundreds of rooms, it did not come close to the Las Vegas megacomplexes with thousands of rooms each, dedicated conference centers, theatres, and enormous pool areas. Such casino-resorts require a car-oriented environment and lots of space, very different from the small lots and pedestrian-centric Macau peninsula.

Casino-hotels also began to colonize Taipa, one of two islands connected to the Macau peninsula with a two-kilometer-long causeway. Still, this residential village had the same spatial constraints as the peninsula. Back in Nevada, the casino-resorts were arranged around a wide, straight automobile highway with room for the Las Vegas Strip to dribble far out in the Mojave Desert. Macau, unlike Las Vegas, is surrounded by the South China Sea.

But in the 1990s, the city had started reclaiming an area called Cotai, a portmanteau of the two islands it connected, Coloane and Taipa. It was meant to be a new town complete with sport, cultural, and educational facilities. But when Las Vegas Sands owner Sheldon Adelson came to look at the new swampland in 2002, he had other plans. He imagined a highway bisecting Cotai lined with mammoth, luxury, resort-style casinos. He wanted a Vegas strip.

In 2007, Adelson opened the Venetian, then the world's largest casino complex, and the Cotai Strip was born. Vegas history repeated itself in Asia, and Macau became the "Vegas of the East." As in 1950s Las Vegas, when the revenue of Strip resorts exceeded the city's smaller downtown casinos, Cotai overtook the peninsula in 2013 as the most popular gaming destination. Cotai's casinos, with thousands of rooms, giant shopping malls, and massive entertainment venues, were far larger than in the peninsula and more profitable. They were also more extravagant. For instance, the skyscrapers of Studio City Macau were inspired by Batman's Gotham City, with two bright "asteroid" holes housing a Ferris wheel. At this writing, with the opening of the $4.1 billion Wynn Palace, the $2.5 billion Parisian, and several other billion-dollar resorts nearing completion, Cotai is bound to become the city's dominant new core. In contrast, the old, colonial Portuguese center stands still in time, congealed according to UNESCO world heritage guidelines.

At first glance, "old" Macau and the new gambling areas may not have much in common. But the former outpost of the Portuguese empire managed to survive on China's doorstep only because it was a place that catered to niche industries, including those that were banned in the region, such as silver, indentured laborers, and gambling.

The effect of the first and longest-lasting encounter between the West and China, from the sixteenth to the twentieth centuries, can be traced in the city's historic core. It holds a mixture of architectural types, a fusion of styles and technologies from different cultures, which led to a UNESCO classification of outstanding heritage value. Now, as foreign as Cotai may seem, it continues Macau's tradition of questionable industries and international exchange.

Fifteen years after breaking the gambling monopoly, what type of city has Macau become? Macau has the world's highest population density, as well as the highest density of casinos. It is a town in which socioeconomic life is increasingly entangled with the casino economy. One sees local families visiting a casino movie theatre or swimming pool, children walk past casino facades on their way to school, fresh graduates find lucrative employment in the casinos, and all citizens receive a bonus from the government as a share of the increasing gaming revenue.

It is also an increasingly cosmopolitan city, with tourists from Hong Kong, Korea, and Japan and tens of thousands of foreign casino workers, including mainland Chinese, Filipinos, and even Gurkhas—Nepalese soldiers known for their toughness—hired as security guards. The city is also dominated by private service industry. For example, the vast network of casino-operated buses, ferries, and helicopters is not geared for locals but to bring visitors across the border to the gambling tables. Macau, a Special Administrative Region built on relaxed licensing requirements, is emblematic of a worldwide trend of what Keller Easterling calls "zones," characterized by extrastate governance and "air-conditioned, infrastructure-rich urbanism that is more familiar to the world than the [local] context."[2]

Macau is a city increasingly fragmented by big-box casino enclaves, most significantly on the Cotai Strip. Their vast, blank exterior walls are so large and have such few entrances it is almost impossible to walk from one to another. Macau has also become a city of spectacle, with a bizarre and truly global medley of free casino-sponsored attractions, including Ponte 16's Michael Jackson Gallery; the Grand Lisboa's collection of precious artifacts; the Grand Emperor's British-style "Changing of the Guard" ceremony; the Galaxy's Korean-pop concerts; the MGM's Murano-glass sculptures; the Venetian's singing gondoliers; and the Wynn's curling animatronic dragon, its nostrils puffing real smoke.

The Architecture of the Casino Complex

This book examines the "casino complex" as both an architectural typology and a dominant industry that reshapes a city to its needs. It highlights the effects of this development in Macau, and raises questions about cultural identity, economic development, architecture, and urban life. We can all learn from Macau as a new frontier of capitalism and a model of urbanism that is as interesting as its counterpart, Las Vegas.

The fourth in a series about contemporary urban forms in China, including *Factory Towns of South China*, *Villages in the City*, and *Mall City*, *Macau and the Casino Complex* explores urban Macau from a multidisciplinary and visual angle.[3] In the second part of this book—the catalog—drawings and photographs show the city's patchwork of distinct urban enclaves, from downtown casinos, whose neon-blasted storefronts eclipse adjacent homes and schools, to the string of isolated palatial complexes along the Cotai Strip. The case studies, arranged by geographic area, reveal the explosive growth of the casino complex to Las Vegas proportions. The evolution of casinos, arranged chronologically in each area, also narrates an escalating race to impress gamblers, beginning with Stanley Ho's precious jade and ivory sculptures at the Lisboa to the New Century's giant statue of thunder-carrying Zeus, and including the Venetian's full-scale replica of the Campanile and the "Vquarium," a vast, video wall teasing tourists with occasional glimpses of a bare-breasted mermaid.

The evolution of the Macau casino complex from gambling hall to megastructure reflects a worldwide trend of expanding building complexes. From Hong Kong's podium-tower estates sprouting above subway stations to Dubai's massive airport terminals that include hotels and offices, the simple building is becoming a complex mini-city, a self-contained world in which tens of thousands of people can live, work, and play. These monoliths radically depart from traditional cities, enfolding every element into one massive object that contains streets, plazas, blocks, and entire buildings.

These built behemoths have arrived stealthily through a gradual convergence of trends in political economy, urbanization patterns, and technological advancements. Neoliberal economies that skew wealth to higher income populations and the private sector have cleared the ground for gated enclaves and privatized landscapes of consumption. Infrastructure nodes and train stations are no longer considered autonomous monuments but are merely a base for even larger buildings. People live and work in climate-controlled interiors, thanks to air-conditioning and electrical lighting, and reach ever-higher floors with faster elevators and escalators.

The megastructures are realizations of the kind of architecture that avant-garde thinkers in earlier eras could only imagine. Futurist Antonio Sant'Elia envisioned *La Città Nuova* ("The New City," published in the *Manifesto of Futurist Architecture*, 1914) as an array of monolithic skyscrapers articulated with snaking lifts and aerial bridges. Modernist pioneer Le Corbusier planned to cut a giant highway megastructure through Algiers in 1931, housing 180,000 people. Back then, all of this remained on the drawing boards. But today, the megastructure has blossomed with a vengeance.

Is there something to be learned from Macau's architecture and urbanism? In 1972, architects Denise Scott Brown and Robert Venturi found architectural lessons in the Las Vegas casinos. They labeled buildings within two opposing semiotic types: the "duck" and the "decorated shed." Ducks—so-named after a Long Island duck egg store shaped like a duck—communicated meaning through their form. In contrast, the shed was a plain, shed-like building whose signage was applied independently, like the Stardust casino, a nondescript building with a huge neon billboard. They discovered that sheds outperformed ducks in the efficient communication of meaning. It was a demonstration of the triumph of symbolic surface over modernist form—a thesis they developed in *Learning from Las Vegas*, a seminal book that signaled the rise of postmodernism.[4]

Today the Stardust is long gone, demolished for a new development, and Las Vegas has ceded the title of the world's casino capital to Macau. Macau is at the cutting edge of leisure architecture, building hotels so enormous they no longer require signage to be noticed. The Venetian Macao[5] and the Galaxy Macau, each covering about a million square meters, are in the world's ten largest buildings by area. Departing from the preliberalization casinos that tend to be "decorated sheds," the megastructures exhibit characteristics of both ducks and sheds: the Venetian and Galaxy communicate meaning through elaborate forms, including Mughal cupolas and a campanile, but also contain elements of sheds, with vast, unpolished patches of back-of-house infrastructure beyond customer viewpoints. The Grand Lisboa merges the duck and shed most clearly: its Fabergé-egg-shape base is also the world's largest integrated LED screen, constantly communicating messages.

Learning from Las Vegas focused on casino architecture as populist iconography of the everyday, documented through "deadpan," drive-by imagery by mounting a camera to the hood of a car. This book understands Macau casino architecture as a corporate production of the everyday, often with hyper-Oriental iconography. It takes a more "forensic" approach that combines formalistic documentation with lived experiences, triangulating interviews with locals with cutaway drawings that reveal zigzagging mazes of marble and escalators.

In the first part of the book, essays provide insight from different disciplines, including architecture, urban planning, geography, anthropology, and business. Contributors give a deeper insight on how the casino complex can be understood in Macau's history of urbanization and gambling, the role of feng shui, and how such projects affect the city's economy and public realm.

In chapter 1, Cathryn Clayton uses the metaphor of the petri dish to capture Macau's urban transformation historically and after the handover. She shows that casino gambling's new dominance is not a radical break but a continuation of Macau's long engagement with the global economy and reliance on niche industries. Such reliance invariably led to rapid growth and sharp declines, shaping Macau through unpredictable cycles of crisis and renewal resulting from a single industry's boom and bust economy. The pattern extends as far back as the sixteenth century, when the Portuguese crown developed a trade base over two decades from a few warehouses to an opulent walled city with churches on every hilltop. Diversity thrived not by purposeful attempt but through the weakness of the state's influence, as Macau was then the farthest-flung piece of the Portuguese empire.

As odd as it may seem to have Venetian canals in a Chinese town, Thomas Daniell writes in chapter 2 how this fits with Macau's history as a "collage city." Investigating its long history of city planning and land reclamation, he recognizes Macau as land that is "authentically" artificial, continuously expanding, constantly modifying. Over half of Macau's current land is reclaimed from the sea, with more to come. This opportunistic expansion strategy led to a different type of city: one that is not a palimpsest of historical layers but a mosaic of adjacent and distinct environments with distinct atmospheres, the different urban patterns reflecting the city's changing ideologies.

Macau's current, spectacular architecture fits perfectly in China's new ideology, as well as the global "society of the spectacle," writes Timothy Simpson in chapter 3. He reveals how the ostentatious and luxurious casino buildings play a role in "consumer pedagogy," training a post-socialist population how to participate in the global consumer economy. If the Shenzhen Special Economic Zone was an experiment with capitalist modes of production, then the Macau Administrative Region should be considered a "laboratory of consumption," where glittering golden buildings and the display of riches stimulate gamblers to try their luck. Macau's shiny and bright-lit casinos, with their green felt tables, thus form a crucial component in the development of capitalism, just as Paris's nineteenth-century arcades once awed and inspired the emerging bourgeoisie with new products, glass roofs, and gaslights.

In chapter 4, urban explorers from HK Urbex unearth one of the first casinos to bring Western casino games and new standards of luxury to Macau. Masterminded by none other than Stanley Ho, the Hotel Estoril opened in 1963 as the city's biggest and most splendiferous casino. Today it faces the wrecking ball. HK Urbex, as well as preservation groups, find meaningful history and beauty in the dilapidated building and its faded futurist mural, the Goddess of Fortune. But the decaying hotel rooms and karaoke parlors are also silent reminders of the transitory nature of development and how the city's new phantasmagoric structures are future ruins.

Kah-Wee Lee uses social history to question professional perception regarding Chinese gamblers in chapter 5. Rather than the "hard-core," pathological gambling drones that western casino consultants and industry experts assume, he examines nineteenth-century Macau and a Chinese town near San Francisco in 1920 to show that gambling was a rich social activity that adapted to different contexts of criminalization and legalization. Lee shows how experts' Orientalist prejudices about Asian gamblers continue to exist and should be seen as an effort to produce types of gambling consumers that further the interest of the casino industry.

In chapter 6, Desmond Lam writes about a type of knowledge influencing gambling and casino design: feng shui, an ancient belief whose advocates posit that the earth, sky, and sea are full of positive and negative *qi* (force), which can be manipulated to improve one's luck. Feng shui "masters" exploit this "science" by offering their services to casino companies. The geomancers try to optimize the perceived "luckiness" of casinos, influencing the design, orientation, and decoration of buildings. For instance, placing pairs of lion statues near the entrance, cladding the structure in gold to express heavenly glory, and coloring interiors predominantly red can generate lots of positive *qi*. On the other hand, most gamblers see feng shui primarily as a tool to extract their money. They hire their own masters to enlarge their good fortune and see through "traps" such as the Wynn's curving slab, interpreted as a knife to cut the "throat" of patrons, and the gold-clad Sands, seen as a beehive, designed to get gamblers' "honey."

From an economic perspective, Miao He and Ricardo Siu show in chapter 7 how the casino complexes by and large have brought fortune to the city of Macau with vast numbers of jobs, all-time low unemployment rates, and swelling tax revenues—even helping Macau weather the 2008 global financial crisis. Nonetheless, the casino influx has also led to domestic inflation, a lowered real standard of living for residents, and rising labor and rental costs for small and medium businesses. Yet, other governments have observed Macau's rise closely. Singapore, Vietnam, the Philippines, and others, were inspired to build their own casino resorts.

Researcher Timothy Luke even speaks of "casinopolitanism," an emergent urban development model that is reshaping several twenty-first-century cities and gaining influence in many places. This model exploits a simulated cosmopolitan allure, which includes among other things celebrity-chef restaurants, luxury shops, and Broadway shows.[6]

The Future of the Casino Complex

What does the future hold for Macau, and where is the casino complex heading? In 2016, Cotai gave birth to three more megaresorts: MGM Cotai, Wynn Palace, and Parisian Macau. The latter boasts a half-size replica of the Eiffel Tower—an unauthorized copy of the casino complex, Paris Las Vegas, which in turn is a copy of the original. In 2018, the $4 billion complex Lisboa Palace is scheduled to open with a yet-unexplored theme: it is modeled after Louis XIV's Palace of Versailles.

Yet Macau is no longer a shrine to replicas alone. The city once predicated its worth on emulating other buildings. The Oceanus casino is a copy of the Beijing Aquatic Stadium—the colorful, bubbly Watercube. Even the city's tallest structure, the 338-meter-tall Macau tower, is a copy of Auckland's Sky Tower, designed by the same architect. But some of the city's new buildings are "originals," designed by celebrated architects. The City of Dreams casino has commissioned a sleek, donut-shaped tower from the mind of famed Zaha Hadid.[7]

Yet, as unique as each of Macau's megastructures may seem, many are marked by sameness. Just as packaging is the only thing that differentiates the essentially identical items on supermarket shelves, architectural themes are used to clad almost identical structures: casino hotels built of post-tensioned concrete slabs and curtain walls, with similarly sized lobbies and double-loaded hotel corridors. Behind the consistency of the megastructure lies the megacorporation, a single entity in charge of a miniature city, each building on the market's dominant model.

Still, more visitors will be Macau bound, thanks to China's growing consumer class and a new fifty-kilometer-long bridge that will connect Macau to Hong Kong. Macau is expected to get so crowded that casino developers are even considering resorts on an entirely different island, Hengqin, which has a hundred-square-kilometer land mass.

Nevertheless, dangers are on the rise. Casino liberalization was intended to cleanse the industry of organized crime—particularly to rid it of the Triad-run junkets that whisk VIP gamblers and their money from the mainland, circumventing the country's strict currency controls. Yet the Triad presence persists. And when the government cracked down on corruption in 2014, revenues began to slide. At the beginning of 2015, Macau's six largest casino operators showed that profits tanked by 49 percent compared to a year earlier, due to a sudden drop in high rollers afraid to attract attention.[8]

Casino liberalization also strained the environment and led to a host of social problems, with increases in gambling-related pathologies, and crime. Even the high school dropout rate increased, due to the low educational requirements of relatively high-paying, casino-related jobs including

card dealers.[9] The government's piecemeal attitude toward planning appears to favor the gaming industry over Macau residents, with casino complexes appropriating spaces meant for public use such as parks. At the same time, growing gambling-related businesses, including souvenir stores and pawnshops, are geared toward tourists, not locals.

Competition is also growing, with potential casino developments in Taiwan and Japan. Further, should the Chinese government decide to tighten visa controls on Chinese customers, the whole Cotai Strip could go back to being a swampland or even underwater. Of all southern Chinese coastal areas, Macau is the most susceptible to climate change and sea level rise because of its ongoing land reclamation.[10]

And Macau still has a few lessons to learn from Las Vegas. The Vegas Strip today derives the majority of revenue from nongaming activities: entertainment, Broadway shows, fine dining, nightclubs, and rooms. Despite efforts to diversify, most of Cotai's revenue is from gambling. Then there is the urban design question of how to string the large casino "enclaves" along an exciting boulevard "armature" (in the terms of urban design theorist David Grahame Shane). A walk along the Las Vegas Strip—arguably the American West's most dynamic pedestrian promenade—brings visitors on a path past spectacular art pieces and world-class architecture. The Cotai Strip, on the other hand, has insulated developments by roads that are virtually impossible to cross, making tourists dependent on buses and taxis.

But unlike Las Vegas, Macau is run by a Chief Executive, who is able to exert substantial influence and control. If one can harness the casino complex and rein in the social and environmental hazards of this volatile industry, it could put Macau on a trajectory to create a more equitable contract between the industry, citizens, and government that is formalized through the built environment, setting an example for other Asian cities eager to add urban gambling. Whether this happens or not, one thing is clear: the casino complex is evolving rapidly and in many ways. Its architectures are transforming, its social dangers are unresolved, its territories are expanding, and its future no longer lies in its birthplace, Las Vegas, but in Macau, the twenty-first-century casino capital.

Notes

1. David Schwartz, *Suburban Xanadu: The Casino Resort on the Las Vegas Strip and Beyond* (New York: Routledge, 2003).

2. Timothy W. Luke, "Casinopolitanism," in *The Wiley-Blackwell Encyclopedia of Globalization*, ed. George Ritzer (Chichester, UK: Wiley-Blackwell, 2012).

3. Stefan Al, ed., *Factory Towns of South China: An Illustrated Guidebook* (Hong Kong: Hong Kong University Press, 2012); Stefan Al, ed., *Villages in the City: A Guide to South China's Informal Settlements* (Hong Kong: Hong Kong University Press, 2014); Stefan Al, ed., *Mall City: Hong Kong's Dreamworlds of Consumption* (Honolulu: University of Hawaii Press, 2016).

4. Robert Venturi, Denise Scott-Brown, and Steven Izenour, *Learning from Las Vegas: The Forgotten Symbolism of Architectural Form* (Cambridge, MA: MIT Press, 1986).

5. The Venetian and the Sands both use "Macao," instead of Macau.

6. Timothy W. Luke, "Casinopolitanism," in *The Wiley-Blackwell Encyclopedia of Globalization*, ed. George Ritzer (Chichester, UK: Wiley-Blackwell, 2012).

7. Las Vegas casino developers too have commissioned famed architects, such as Daniel Libeskind. See Stefan Al, *The Strip: Las Vegas and the Architecture of the American Dream* (Cambridge, MA: MIT Press, 2017).

8. Kate O'Keeffe, "China Corruption Crackdown Deals Macau a Rough Hand," *Wall Street Journal*, 3 March 2015.

9. Yim King Penny Wan, Xin Crystal Li, and Weng Hang Kong, "Social Impacts of Casino Gaming in Macau: A Qualitative Analysis," *Tourism: An International Interdisciplinary Journal* 59:1 (2011), 63–82.

10. Lin Wang, Huang Gang, Zhou Wen, and Chen Wen, "Historical Change and Future Scenarios of Sea Level Rise in Macau and Adjacent Waters," *Advances in Atmospheric Sciences* 33:4 (2016), 462–475, doi:10.1007/s00376-015-5047-1.

CASINO HEIGHTS

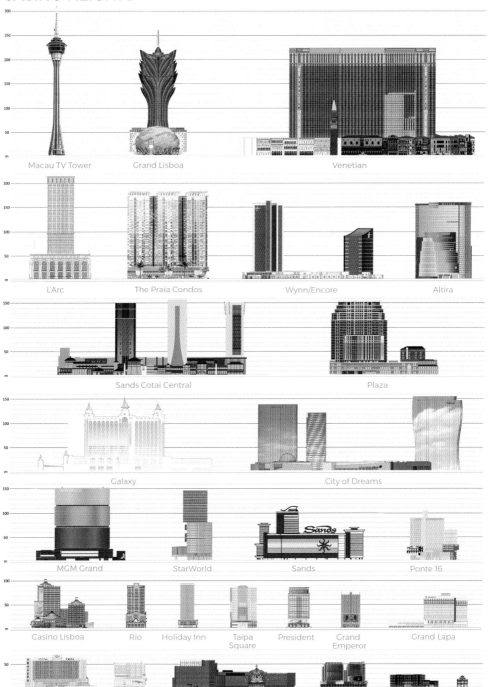

Macau TV Tower

Grand Lisboa

Venetian

L'Arc

The Praia Condos

Wynn/Encore

Altira

Sands Cotai Central

Plaza

Galaxy

City of Dreams

MGM Grand

StarWorld

Sands

Ponte 16

Casino Lisboa

Rio

Holiday Inn

Taipa Square

President

Grand Emperor

Grand Lapa

New Century

Casa Real

Broadway

Golden Dragon

Casino Babylon

The Ruins of St. Paul's Church

GLOBAL GAMING REVENUE 2001–2014 (US$ MILLION)

MACAU
LAS VEGAS
ATLANTIC CITY
SINGAPORE*

Thirteen years after casino liberalization in 2002, Macau had multiplied its gaming revenue eighteen fold to $44 billion, seven times the revenue of Las Vegas.

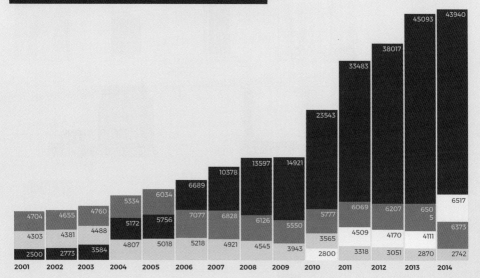

	2001	2002	2003	2004	2005	2006	2007	2008	2009	2010	2011	2012	2013	2014
Macau	2500	2773	3584	4807	5756	6689	10378	13597	14921	23543	33483	38017	45093	43940
	4303	4381	4488	5172	5218	7077	6828	6126	5550	5777	6069	6207	6505	6517
	4704	4655	4760	5334	6034	5018	4921	4545	3943	3565	4509	4170	4111	6373
										2800	3318	3051	2870	2742

*Singapore officially opened its first casino 14 Feb. 2010,

Source: Center for Gaming Research.
University of Nevada, Las Vegas

Infographic by Feng Yizhou

GLOBAL GAMING REVENUE RATIO 2001–2014

MACAU
LAS VEGAS
ATLANTIC CITY
SINGAPORE*

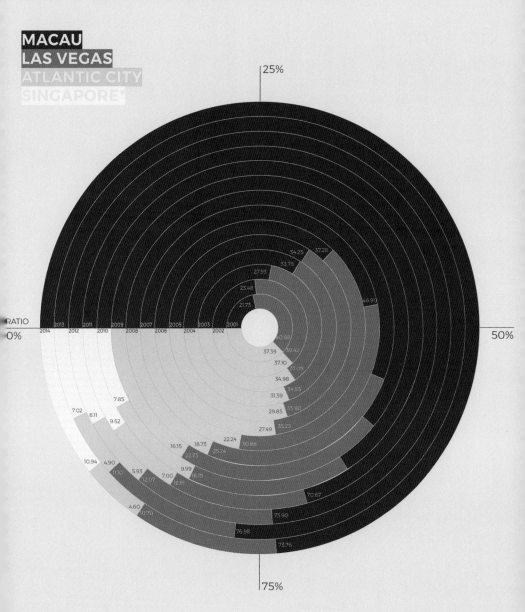

25%

RATIO

0%

2014 2013 2012 2011 2010 2009 2008 2007 2006 2005 2004 2003 2002 2001

50%

75%

34.25   37.28
33.78
27.93
23.48
21.73
40.88
37.39   39.42
37.10   37.09
34.98   34.83
31.39
29.85   35.90
27.49   35.23
22.24
18.73   25.24   30.86
16.15   22.73
9.99   16.19   12.81
7.00
5.93   12.07
11.10   4.90
10.94
10.70   4.60
46.90
70.67
73.90
76.98
73.76
7.85
7.02   8.11   9.52

CHAPTER 1
PETRI-DISH URBANISM

CATHRYN H. CLAYTON

"Macau is like a petri dish."

Almost twenty years ago now, a Chinese acquaintance of mine (let us call him Kwan), born and raised in Macau, gave me that image with which to think about his city. It was the late 1990s, a year or two before Macau's transfer from Portuguese to Chinese administration, and I was living in Macau, working at a local foundation and doing ethnographic fieldwork for my dissertation on cultural identity and political transition.

I was asking as many people as I could what, if anything, made Macau different from other Chinese cities. For this young man, the petri-dish image evoked something essential about Macau—the sense of both containment and diversity peculiar to daily life in a city that had, for over 400 years, existed on the shifting edges of overlapping empires and economies. It was small space, constrained by the sea on three sides and a closely patrolled border on the fourth. But in this space many different "organisms" had found fertile ground, such that each of them, as he put it, "keeps expanding upward and inward, and all their differences get magnified."

As I have returned to Macau time and again over the years (first to teach at the University of Macau from 2001–2005, and afterwards for extended visits every year or so), I have continued to find Kwan's image a useful way of thinking about urban change and cultural identity in twenty-first century Macau. First, because its resonances with other concepts that have been used to analyze contemporary Asian cities reveals the unique aspects of what appears to be a generic process of urban change and differentiation. Second,

because it is this kind of petri-dish urbanism that some residents and observers of Macau fear may be disappearing with the advent of the casino complex. And third, because the tropes of expansion and magnification can help us to think more dynamically about urban change and continuity, culture, and identity, across time.

The petri-dish simile is, of course, hardly a new one in the study of cities. Rem Koolhaas uses the phrase to describe the apparent memorylessness of what he terms the "Generic City": the apotheosis of contemporary urban space, in which "almost any hypothesis can be 'proven' and then erased, never again to reverberate in the minds of its authors or audience" (Koolhaas 1995:1255). This is not how Kwan meant it. Indeed, there are many ways in which a petri dish is not a good simile for Macau. The implication of a white-coated scientist hovering nearby, intentionally cultivating certain carefully selected organisms under sterile and closely controlled conditions, does not reflect the role of historical accident and human agency in shaping the culture and boundaries of any city, especially Macau. Certainly in Macau those boundaries have proven simultaneously more porous and less transparent than the smooth, clear, impermeable walls of a cell culture dish. And in the context of the biology laboratory, unlike in Macau, the accidental interaction or admixture between two strains can only be thought of in negative terms, as "contamination."

What Kwan intended to emphasize was, rather, the laissez-faire nature of the petri dish—throw some bacteria in a cell culture dish, put on the lid, and leave it alone for a few days—as well as the chaotic and claustrophobic feeling that resulted. This was in stark contrast to the image of Macau that the Portuguese and Chinese governments were promoting at the time. Theirs was the image of the bridge, in which the intimacy of Macau's urban spaces had led not to the magnification of differences but to the attenuation of difference through interaction, hybridization, and the "blending of East and West."

Yet the image of Macau as petri dish—in which many distinct and self-contained colonies of organisms grow together in one small space— was the one that resonated more deeply with many Macau residents I spoke to in the late 1990s. Those who remembered Macau in the early and mid-twentieth century recalled more or less distinct ethnic neighborhoods—the Macanese in Lilau, the Portuguese in Barra, and the Cantonese along the Inner Harbour and up to the Border Gate. But, due to the small size of the city, these communities regularly rubbed shoulders in public spaces, and the well being of each depended on that of the others.

By the 1990s, population growth meant that only vestiges of those distinct neighborhoods remained. Spatially, the colonies had grown into each other, making the distinctions between communities social rather than geographic. As one Portuguese acquaintance put it in 1998, it was as if there were multiple cities within the confines of one little urban footprint.[1] It was this plurality of urbanisms that the petri-dish metaphor expressed so concretely: the sense that several cities occupied the same physical space, each with its own linguistic, economic, and cultural identity, each one nourished by different elements of a shared nutrient mix, growing and changing shape and shifting position in relation to the others, sometimes dominating the landscape and at others getting crowded out of existence.

In its emphasis on codependent diversity, Kwan's invocation of the petri dish seems to have more in common with Koolhaas's notion of the "City of Exacerbated Difference©," a form of urbanism that does not strive for balance and homogeneity but is "based on the greatest possible difference between its parts" and on "the opportunistic exploitation of flukes, accidents, and imperfections" (Koolhaas in Chung et al., *Great Leap Forward*:29). According to Koolhaas, although such urban formations appear chaotic, they in fact form a delicate system in which "the slightest modification of any detail requires the readjustment of the whole to reassert the equilibrium of complementary extremes" (Chung et al. 2001:29).

The COED© concept was advanced as a model to explain the new urban formations engulfing the Pearl River Delta (PRD) region just to Macau's north. Yet aspects of the COED© certainly find echoes in Macau, and it is especially useful in conceptualizing Macau's position within the broader PRD region in the years since the handover. But this model assumes the self-conscious engineering of difference in response to the call of a highly ideological state. In short, it suggests an authority, or series of authorities, who defines the identities and boundaries of each of the various parts and then cultivates (or encourages others to cultivate) difference between them.[2] By contrast, the twentieth-century process of magnification that Kwan was talking about did not arise from deliberate experimentation or from a purposeful attempt to encourage diversity as a strategy of capital accumulation. Rather, it resulted from the very weakness of the modern Macau state and its capacity for standardization and systematization.

For centuries, Macau was the farthest-flung piece of a global Portuguese empire, a tiny peninsula clinging to the southern edge of the vast Qing realm, and a trade entrepôt located along East Asia's busiest shipping lanes. As a result, people and commodities from Europe, Africa, South and Southeast Asia, Latin America, Japan, Korea, and many parts of China found their way to Macau through their own volition or otherwise.[3]

During most of the twentieth century, the city's official language was spoken by less than 5 percent of the population; there was no public school system for the 95 percent of school-age children whose mother tongue was Chinese;

no unified history curriculum, no attempts to inculcate in residents a sense of belonging to the city or allegiance to any overarching state ideology; and few urban plans that outlasted the tenure of any single governor. The Portuguese state in Macau looked after its own citizens, who accounted for only about 3 percent of Macau residents. For the rest, Chinese civic organizations stepped into the breach. Native-place organizations, lineage organizations, labor unions, guilds, charities run by the Kuomintang (Nationalist Party), mutual aid associations run by the Communist Party, as well as Catholic, Protestant, Buddhist, Baha'i and other religious institutions ran schools and provided the social services and senses of community and identity that the state did not. In doing so, they did not just perpetuate but actively strengthened a wide range of distinct but overlapping forms of social, political, cultural, and linguistic identification among Macau residents.

In short, radical heterogeneity and a kind of contained and delicate chaos are hardly new in Macau. What does seem new is the deliberate attempt to sort and separate this heterogeneity, both conceptually and spatially.

. . .

This book is based on the premise that the casino complex is a distinct form of urbanism in which a single industry has, in the period since the gaming sector was opened to competition in 2001, remade the city of Macau in its own image. As the essays in this book show, the changes wrought by the casino complex are to be found not just on the skyline and in the economy but in forms of political engagement, quality of life, consumer preferences, patterns of movement, and expectations of "the good life." Observers have emphasized the transformative and totalizing nature of this process. Some laud it as the opening up of a seedy, corrupt, and closed society to the fresh air of globalization. Others malign it as evidence of the relentless speed and potency with which corporate capital creates new frontiers of exploitation and accumulation at the expense of just about everything else. In both cases, there is a sense that new regulatory mechanisms, new urban infrastructures, and new market forces are homogenizing, standardizing, integrating (both internally and externally), and differentiating the city to an extent that the state has never before managed, or even cared, to do.

For many Macau residents, too, this narrative of sudden, transformative impact rings true. The speed of economic, political, and social change has opened previously unthinkable opportunities for some while creating pressures that many others find difficult to endure. For most, the effects of this change are inescapable. Economically speaking, residents have witnessed seemingly impossible growth rates that have given them, by some calculations, one of the highest per capita GDPs in the world.

Yet, especially in the wake of the 2009 downturn, when one of the two largest casino operators teetered on the edge of bankruptcy and laid off 11,000 employees, there is a heightened awareness of the unstable, boom-and-bust nature of this prosperity. The high wages paid by casinos have changed the employment structure. Government bureaus, foundations, nonprofits, even restaurants and others in the service industry have had their most capable junior staff "poached" by casinos hungry and willing to pay top dollar for talented, experienced, bi- or tri-lingual local employees. Casino liberalization has changed the aspirations of Macau's youth: high school students who might have once aspired to a college education and a career in business or public service can now earn more straight out of high school as dealers, and at the University of Macau the major in Gaming Management regularly attracts the best students.

Yet even these high wages have not been able to keep up with the skyrocketing real estate prices, driven by investment and speculation from Hong Kong and mainland China. Although the government has built more public housing to accommodate low-income residents, young middle-class couples planning to marry and start a family are having to either delay doing so until they can save enough for a down payment or buy a condominium across the border in Zhuhai and commute through the immigration checkpoint every day.

At the same time, many feel that their options have narrowed: career paths outside the casino and entertainment sector that will pay enough for a young family to live a relatively comfortable middle-class life are becoming increasingly difficult to find, while even within that sector, competition from the huge numbers of imported workers (some 28 percent of the labor force now hails from outside of Macau) make salary increases, promotions, and job-hopping opportunities increasingly difficult to secure.[4] The high profile corruption case in 2008 of the Secretary for Transport and Public Works, Ao Man Long, who was convicted of accepting over U.S.$3 million in kickbacks from the construction of projects such as the Venetian and Galaxy StarWorld (among others), shook public faith in the city's post-handover political leaders and laid bare the troubling extent of collusion between the state and private capital. While it may be that these changes were foreseeable and temporary signs of an economy in transition, they have led some residents to lament that the small-town, intimate sensibility they once enjoyed in Macau is being replaced by a more competitive, exploitative, materialistic ethos. Less like a petri dish, more like a cattle car.

These economic developments are manifest through equally transformative changes to the urban environment. The casino boom has brought a population boom (from around 430,000 in 1999 to around 600,000 in 2016), which has in turn necessitated a boom in construction of high-rise condominium towers and public housing blocks in neighborhoods throughout the city. Automobile traffic on the narrow downtown streets has become a knotted mess: the sharp rise in population and in the number of tourists (from around 7 million per year in the late 1990s to 31 million in 2014) has strained public transportation, while new employment, housing, and traffic patterns mean that increasing numbers of residents feel the need (and have the means) to own private cars.

The most spectacular changes to Macau's cityscape, however, have happened at a distance from the most densely populated residential areas: the construction of the casinos themselves —buildings on a scale previously unthinkable in a space as small as Macau—on massive tracts of landfill conjoining what were once two separate islands. Whereas in the pre-2001 era, Macau's ten casinos were all within easy walking distance of some of the most densely populated parts of the peninsula, the Cotai Strip is designed to be most easily reached by bus or automobile. Indeed, one of the principal changes that distinguishes the casino complex in Macau is the expansion of automobile urbanism: unlike the narrow roadways and pedestrian-only zones that make it easier to walk than drive on the Macau peninsula, the Cotai Strip is ringed by

intersecting six-lane, high-speed thoroughfares where the paucity of crosswalks and absence of stoplights facilitate the quick movement of cars and buses to and from the border and residential areas in the north (where many casino workers live) but constrain pedestrians' ability to move between the casinos and the closest, newest residential areas on Taipa, just across the street.[5]

In this regard, it appears that one of the main effects of casino development is the exacerbation of the difference between Macau's gaming economy and its historical and cultural identity. For decades, Macau has relied on both its casinos and its architectural heritage as resources for economic development. For many, it was the juxtaposition of the two—the "churches alongside brothels," in W. H. Auden's words—that contributed to the city's petri-dish sensibility.[6] But the increasing dependence on the casino sector has led the Macau government to pursue cultural tourism as a means of economic diversification (Tam 2014:306). This has led to the spatial and conceptual separation and purification of these two aspects of the Macau experience: the "old Macau", intimate cradle of culture and identity, versus the "gambling city", exemplified by the Cotai Strip, a vast "cultural desert" that trades on its ability to detach markers of cultural identity (the Venetian?) from any possible sense of belonging.

The "Old City": crowded outdoor street markets; cobblestone plazas; quiet churches; narrow, crooked lanes lined with stalls selling cheap factory overruns of textiles from China; rundown shops whose rows of salt fish hanging from the ceiling and sacks of dried medicinal herbs crowding the storefront advertise themselves to the noses of passers-by long before they come into view; back-alley shrines to local deities; and quiet parks where elderly men walk their birds at sunrise. Here, carefully cultivated signs of "history" and "local culture" permeate the outdoor spaces, and the pedestrian has the distinct advantage.

The gambling city: air-conditioned simulacra of street markets; wide hallways lined with boutiques selling brand-name European and American merchandise; ventilation systems that whisk away unsettling smells; and back alleys accessible only to the maintenance crew. Here, pedestrian space is largely indoor space. It can take longer to walk from one end of the Venetian to the other than to walk from Leal Senado to the São Paulo Ruins. Even the walkways that connect neighboring casinos to each other and to Taipa Village are enclosed, and great care has been taken to anonymize the environment. The premise of this division both rests on and reinforces the idea that, to paraphrase Koolhaas again, the past is the locus of authenticity and identity, while the new can only ever be a generic replica of somewhere else. Old and new both have their pleasures, but it seems they can no longer be experienced simultaneously.

. . .

Does the advent of these systematic attempts to exacerbate and commodify the differences between Macau's parts spell the end of its petri-dish urbanism? This is an open question. But it is also not a new one. For the past century at least, the idea that the cultural identity of Macau and its residents has been largely defined, even determined, by the city's urban landscape—and the concern that changes to that landscape are spelling the end of whatever it is that makes Macau unique—has been a recurring refrain. In the 1990s, as real estate speculation sparked a boom in high-rise construction and made land reclamation a highly profitable enterprise (in Macau as in the rest of the Pearl River Delta), many local residents lamented the disappearance of the "sleepy old small-town Macau" and feared that the urban fabric that had made Macau such a fascinating and distinctive city—the crooked crisscrossing of lanes and alleyways, the multicolored jumble of low-slung, multipurpose buildings—was disappearing under the weight of giant, generic housing blocks. And some seventy years earlier still, Portuguese writer and Macau resident Manuel da Silva Mendes decried the destruction of that which defined "our very being, our life, our history": a city comprised of distinct Chinese and Portuguese neighborhoods, each designed in accordance with distinctly Chinese and Portuguese aesthetics and usages in mind but coexisting comfortably in one city. As a new, modern urbanism that emphasized rationalism, connectivity, and openness took hold in Macau, these older neighborhoods were cut down, sometimes slowly and sometimes almost overnight, to make way for buildings and roadways that Silva Mendes felt rendered Macau "an architectonic confusion, characterless, contemptible."[7]

There is irony here, of course. Some the very buildings that Silva Mendes found so characterless and contemptible are quite likely those that have today been classified as cultural heritage sites (such as those that line the Avenida de Almeida Ribeiro, or "New Street," built in the early twentieth century just around the time that Silva Mendes wrote this dirge for his adopted city), prized by at least some residents as symbols of all that defines Macau's being, its life, and its history and protected by the government against encroachment by new forms of "architectonic confusion" represented by the Grand Lisboa and Macau Fisherman's Wharf. But this irony is also the point. In each case, these concerns have been unfounded, not because changes to the urban landscape have no impact on cultural identity but precisely because both cities and cultural identities are dynamic things that are constantly in process of redefinition.

What such static spatial analyses do not consider is how residents make new meanings out of urban spaces, often blurring the spatial and ideological boundaries between them. Prior to 2001, with few exceptions, the old casinos were dedicated to gambling, pure and simple. Yet despite the casinos' spatial proximity to the urban core, many Macau residents lived their entire lives hardly ever setting foot into them. The casinos functioned almost purely as tourist spaces. The new casino-entertainment complexes, by contrast, incorporate air-conditioned shopping malls selling both luxury and midrange global brands, cinemas playing first-run films in state-of-the-art theaters, and concert venues that feature performers from Asia, Europe, and North America. Not long ago, Macau residents would have had to go to Hong Kong to enjoy such entertainment and consumer facilities. The new complexes—although farther from the city center than the old casinos—attract locals and tourists alike and are thus more closely integrated within urban life for a broader spectrum of Macau residents.

At the same time, spaces that were once used and enjoyed equally by residents and tourists alike, such as Leal Senado Square, have become almost exclusively tourist spaces. Sudden rent hikes and the loss of staff to casinos in the mid-2000s meant that locally owned shops that once did brisk local business in the square's historic buildings and had been old favorites for decades—such as the stationer's that could be counted on to stock both postcards and local schoolbooks, the music and video shop that sold a quirky selection of old black-and-white Chinese films and 1940s jazz, the inexpensive vegetarian cafeteria run by a local Buddhist association, and several restaurants, cafes, noodle shops, and ice cream vendors—were forced out, replaced by Starbucks, McDonalds, Watson's, and retailers catering to mainland tourists. Hong Kong-based cosmetics retailer SaSa opened three separate outlets within 200 meters of each other between Leal Senado and the São Paulo Ruins. This gives the lie to the notion that heritage buildings are any less generic, or any more expressive of local identities, than the casino-entertainment complexes.[8]

. . .

In many ways, then, Macau today is a very different city than it was at the time of the handover. But by highlighting this contrast, we may miss a more dynamic perspective and a different way of conceptualizing what makes Macau Macau. From this perspective, the casino complex appears less a definitive break with the past than the latest chapter in an old story. It is not so much an erasure of Macau identity as a magnification of certain aspects of that identity. It is possible here to see continuity where others see change—the continuation of Macau's long-standing role as a niche economy, small and flexible enough to be able to organize quickly and profitably around a single activity. It is precisely this characteristic that has enabled the casino complex to achieve such dizzying success in Macau in the first place.

In fact, the phenomenon of a single industry shaping the political, economic, social, and physical space of the city to meet its own needs can be said to have characterized much of Macau's entire history as a city. After all, it was deliberately established in the mid-sixteenth century for the sole purpose of international trade. And collusion between state and private (global) capital has always been a crucial part of this story. For about eighty years in the sixteenth and seventeenth centuries, Macau functioned as a node in the global trade networks managed by the Portuguese crown. In the space of about two decades, it grew from a few mat-sheds on the landing between two fishing villages into a walled city with churches on every hilltop and fortresses on every bay, its opulence recounted by Chinese poets and playwrights and whose wealth and position was the envy of European monarchs. This, too, was a boom-and-bust economy. The conditions that had enabled Macau's spectacular rise in the sixteenth century disappeared almost as quickly in the middle of the seventeenth, and the city shrank with it. As the features of this "trade complex" changed over time—the trading partners involved, the commodities being bought and sold, the uses to which the massive profits were put—these historical shifts were recorded in the urban landscape. Street names such as Parsee Road, Holland Park Avenue, Coolie Place, and Moors' Extension and buildings such as the São Paulo ruins, the Opium House, and the Lou Kau mansion exist today long after the communities and commodities they represented have disappeared from daily life.

Today, casino liberalization has exacerbated this niche economy, making the livelihoods of Macau residents more dependent on a single industry than ever (the proportion of Macau residents employed in nongaming-related industries is well under 20 percent), while shortening the periods of the boom-and-bust cycles. It has also ensured that the city is more closely integrated into regional and global economic orders than ever. By reframing the story of Macau's current transformation in terms of continuity with the past, I do not mean to suggest that the casino complex is just a matter of history repeating itself or to discount the sensibilities of those residents who find such changes disorienting or worse. But in order to more fully appreciate the dynamics and limits of the casino complex, it is useful to recall that, in many ways, they represent an intensification of Macau's long history as a site for engagements with the global economy in which successive, dominant industries have created and sustained a city where cycles of boom and bust, crisis and renewal have shaped and reshaped the urban environment, never quite predictably.

As more local residents find more reasons to bridge the new geographical and ideological separation between "old" and "new" Macau, expanding the boundaries of their city and incorporating new forms of diversity into their daily lives, will we witness the end of petri-dish urbanism, or its rebirth?

Notes

1. I discuss the comments of this Portuguese acquaintance, and the petri-dish metaphor, in greater depth in *Sovereignty at the Edge: Macau and the Question of Chineseness* (Cambridge, MA: Harvard University Asia Center, 2009).

2. Most of the insightful essays in Chung et al., *Great Leap Forward*, reference ways in which the Chinese state, at various levels, either directly plans or indirectly encourages, manipulates, or exploits urbanization in the Pearl River Delta. The book's title is perhaps no coincidence, referencing one of the modern Chinese state's most centralized, invasive, ideological, and catastrophic attempts at socioeconomic planning.

3. Soldiers and priests and governors were posted there; slaves, convicts, and orphaned girls were sent there; indentured Chinese laborers on their way elsewhere stopped off there, and refugees from inland conflicts took shelter there.

4. Zheng and Hung 2012.

5. By contrast, the casino-hotels that have been built on the Macau peninsula, such as the Grand Lisboa, the Wynn, the Waldo, the Sands, and Ponte 16 are a short walk from the old city center but for the most part are surrounded by multilane roadways and parking areas that separate them from residential areas and constrain pedestrian access.

6. Auden 1939:13–14.

7. Manuel da Silva Mendes, Manuel da Silva Mendes: a instrução pública em Macau (Macau, Direcção dos serviços de educação e juventude, 1996). For a discussion of the modernist urbanism being introduced to Macau at the time, see Margarida Saraiva, "Um jovem romantico, uma nova avenida e um beco sem saída," Hoje Macau, 1 September 2010 (http://hojemacau.com.mo/?p=1761).

8. This is not to say that local residents do not value architectural heritage. A 2009 survey showed that the government's decision to pursue UNESCO heritage status for the Macau Historical Centre was one of its most popular policies since the handover (Clayton 2014). On numerous occasions since 2007, the Macau government has been forced to change its plans to demolish or alter various heritage structures on the Macau peninsula in response to vociferous public opposition (see Tam 2014).

References

Auden, W. H. 1939. "Macao." In *Journey to a War*, by Christopher Isherwood and W. H. Auden. New York: Random House.

Chung, Judy Chuihua, Jeffrey Inaba, Rem Koolhaas, and Sze Tsung Leong, eds. 2001. *Great Leap Forward*. Köln: Taschen.

Clayton, Cathryn H. 2009. *Sovereignty at the Edge: Macau and the Question of Chineseness*. Cambridge, MA: Harvard University Asia Center.

———. 2014. "Macao Local, Macao Global." In *China's Macao Transformed: Challenge and Development in the 21st Century*, Eilo W. Y. Yu and Ming K. Chan, eds., pp. 381–404. Hong Kong: City University of Hong Kong Press.

Koolhaas, Rem. 1995. "The Generic City." In *S, M, L, XL*, by Rem Koolhaas and Bruce Mau, Jennifer Sigler ed., pp. 1248–1264. Rotterdam: 010 Publ.

Mendes, Manuel da Silva. 1996. Manuel da Silva *Mendes: a instrução pública em Macau*. Macau, Direcção dos Serviços de Educação e Juventude.

Saraiva, Margarida. 2010. "Um jovem romantico, uma nova avenida e um beco sem saída," Hoje Macau, 1 September 2010 (http://hojemacau.com.mo/?p=1761).

Tam, Derrick. 2014. "Heritage Protection, Tourism and Urban Planning in Macau." In *China's Macao Transformed*, Eilo W. Y. Yu and Ming K. Chan, eds., pp 297–332. Hong Kong: City University of Hong Kong Press.

Zheng, Victor, and Eva Hung. 2012. *"Evaluating the Economic Impact of Casino Liberalization in Macao," Journal of Gambling Studies* 28(3):541–559.

URBAN MORPHOLOGY, 1557-2014

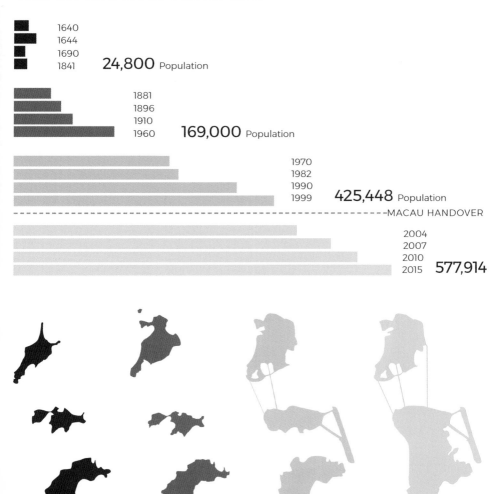

1640
1644
1690
1841 **24,800** Population

1881
1896
1910
1960 **169,000** Population

1970
1982
1990
1999 **425,448** Population
--MACAU HANDOVER

2004
2007
2010
2015 **577,914**

1557-1840   1840-1974   1974-1999   1999-2014

Source: Briefing of Macau City
Development, 2010, Land, Public Works,
and Transport Bureau of the Macau SR

Infographic by Toby Mei Yan Cheung

MACAU
PENINSULA

TAIPA

COTAI

COLOANE

N

Land area 1557 (11.6 sqkm)
Land area 2016 (29.9 sqkm)

CHAPTER 2
UNCOMMON
GROUND

THOMAS DANIELL

"Enough shovels of earth: a mountain. Enough pails of water: a river."

—Chinese proverb

Huge architectural enclaves within a tiny territorial enclave, the new "integrated resorts" (or "casino complexes") that now dominate Macau's visual and cultural identity contain isolated, climate-controlled interiors within iconic, spectacularly illuminated exteriors. Their flamboyant facades belie the introversion of their planning: the casinos themselves are sequestered deep inside, buffered from the street by arcades of luxury shops complemented by hotels, restaurants, bars, nightclubs, cinemas, theaters, galleries, swimming pools, gymnasiums, play areas for children, and so on. Most integrated resorts cover an entire city block, but each has only a couple of public entrances, serviced by fleets of complimentary buses and taxis shuttling between the airport, the ferry terminals, the border crossings to China, and the other casinos.

On the Macau peninsula, the main integrated resorts (Sands Macao, Wynn, MGM Grand, StarWorld, L'Arc, Rio, Fortuna, Golden Dragon, Grand Emperor, Grand Lapa, Grand Lisboa) sit among streets suffused with a lurid LED nimbus from rows of money-laundering pawnshops and stores dealing in watches, jewelry, electronics, luxury clothing, and rare Chinese medicines. But the main integrated resorts in the offshore Cotai area (Sands Cotai Central, MGM Cotai,

Wynn Palace, Galaxy Macau, City of Dreams, Studio City, Plaza Casino, Venetian Macao, Parisian Macao) are surrounded by nothing at all. No shops or restaurants exist independent of their casino hosts. Disengaged from, if not actively inhibiting, everyday street life, Cotai's integrated resorts are designed using exotic styles that explicitly and emphatically avoid any relationship with local history or context.

Arguably, this is a perfectly valid approach, in that there is no context or history to speak of here. Cotai consists entirely of artificial land reclaimed since the turn of the millennium, so the integrated resorts have been designed with the freedom afforded by what is effectively a blank slate allowing the realization of the most extreme architectural fantasies without the usual civic constraints.

Despite all their vulgar artifice, such insular, contrived, controlled nonplaces must be accepted as a legitimate, if not definitive, aspect of postcolonial Macau. In fact, given the cumulative impact of the artificial creation of the land, the artificial utopias of the integrated resorts, and the artificial political status of the Special Administrative Region, it seems that the authenticity of this place now lies in its artificiality.

Sanctioned and leased by China to Portugal in 1557 as a base for international trade and religious proselytization, Macau eventually came to be seen as a de facto Portuguese colony. At the time of its return to China in 1999, it was the last vestige of the Portuguese colonial empire. Its status was always somewhat ambiguous, simultaneously independent from yet reliant on China. In a 1961 speech, Portugal's then-prime minister, António de Oliveira Salazar asserted,

> This province has known periods of prosperity and decadence. As it cannot expand, it suffers from natural limitations. The existence of Macau is based on old treaties celebrated between the Portuguese kings and the Chinese emperors… If we don't respect the legality of these treaties, it would be sure that Macau, in spite of our resistance, would end up being absorbed into China, on which this province entirely depends for its daily existence.[1]

Nonetheless, following the Carnation Revolution of 1974, Portugal began trying to return Macau to China. The offer was initially declined, but in 1987 the two nations signed the Joint Declaration on the Question of Macau, which set out the terms for a transfer of sovereignty. Macau, like Hong Kong, would become a Special Administrative Region for fifty years before being fully integrated into mainland China.

However, when the transfer took place, the Chinese received far more than they had given away. Generously described as a peninsula, Macau was a less-than-3 square kilometer protuberance from the southwest coastline of the Pearl River Delta when the Portuguese arrived. By the early twentieth century it was 11 square kilometers; in the mid-1980s it was 16 square kilometers; and by 1999, the year of its return to China, Macau had reached 24 square kilometers.[2] At the time of writing, Macau is almost 30 square kilometers, a 1,000 percent increase from its original size. While much of this was achieved by expanding the territorial borders to incorporate existing land, more than half of the current area was reclaimed from the sea, and new landfill projects are underway.

Macau's evolving identity may have originated in a historical hybridization of different cultures, but it is being enabled by the ongoing expansion and modification of its territorial borders. The material results are easily visible in maps and aerial photographs, as each successive expansion has a distinctive grain of street patterns and building morphology. Land reclamation in Macau has a long and tortuous history, overdetermined by political exigencies, economic crises, demographic pressures, and cultural ambitions. The result is an erratic series of well-intentioned projects that were all too often cancelled, compromised, or abandoned while still incomplete. Though casinos presently occupy a major proportion of the reclaimed land, they have never been the primary intention, always an expedient, remedial solution to a lack of immediate economic success.

Geographically and geologically, Macau was a small archipelago of granite outcroppings that centuries of silting gradually merged into a single mass, connected to the Chinese mainland by a long isthmus.[3] The earliest significant land reclamation projects were triggered by the sudden decline of Macau's economy in the mid-nineteenth century following centuries of easy prosperity. Soon after Hong Kong became a British colony, ceded in 1842 at the end of the Opium Wars, Macau lost its status as the region's primary mercantile port. International trading companies, together with their employees and families, abandoned Macau in favor of the larger and deeper harbor of Hong Kong and the presumed superior efficiency of British bureaucracy.

To improve government revenue, the Portuguese administration diversified the economy into opium processing, regulated prostitution, and the "coolie" indentured worker trade, as well as launching two policies that would prove to be decisive for Macau's future. Gambling, which had existed in Macau in various unregulated forms since the sixteenth century, was officially sanctioned, thereby enabling its taxation. Trade, which had made Macau the richest place in the world for three centuries, was in decline, so the Portuguese government commissioned feasibility studies for improving sea access and expanding the available land area.

In 1846, the new governor, João Maria Ferreira do Amaral, unilaterally declared Macau to be an independent Portuguese colony. He then laid claim to two islands to the south of the peninsula, Coloane and Taipa—the latter actually comprised two immediately adjacent islands called Taipa Grande and Taipa Pequena, which

Arquitectonica, City of Dreams, 2009. Courtesy City of Dreams

View of the Cotai Strip. Photo: Luís Almoster

were unified by land reclamation in the 1950s. He also consolidated the Portuguese presence on the large islands to the west, Xiao Hengqin and Da Hengqin (known in Portuguese as Dom João and Montanha respectively, during the 1990s China expanded and merged them into what is now called simply Hengqin Island).

In 1848, Amaral ordered the eradication of a zone of squatter shacks, pig farms, and garbage dumps that had accumulated near the border between Macau and China. Despite being on the Macau side of the border gate, this area was recognized as being under China's jurisdiction, and residents paid land tax to the Chinese authorities. Amaral decreed it to be Portuguese territory, with rent to be paid his administration. The residents objected, and the Chinese authorities put a price on Amaral's head, literally. In 1849, he was assassinated, his head and hand sent as trophies to the authorities in Guangzhou.[4] The territorial conflict was eventually resolved by the signing of the 1887 Sino-Portuguese Treaty of Amity and Commerce, which gave Portugal "perpetual occupation and government" over the Macau peninsula and "its dependencies," an implicit acknowledgment of Portuguese control of Coloane and Taipa, though not of the two Hengqin Islands.

Macau's main seaport at the time was the Porto Interior (Inner Harbor), located on the west side of the peninsula. Incessant silting had made it inaccessible to larger boats, so remedial work was begun along the entire west coast. Sea walls and landfill were used to smooth and straighten the ragged edges, incidentally creating Macau's first neighborhoods of regularly aligned streets and building lots. In 1883, Portuguese engineer Adolfo Ferreira de Loureiro was dispatched to Macau in order to plan and supervise a complete overhaul of the Porto Interior. After extensive hydrographic and geographic surveys, he produced a proposal to dredge the harbor, create new maritime channels, and reconfigure the coastlines of the peninsula and Taipa to prevent future silting. This was summarily rejected by the Macau government as too expensive, though they declined a loan offered by a French syndicate to pay for the work in return for a temporary monopoly on gambling and some land on which to build hotels and casinos.[5] Over the next three decades, Ferreira and various others proposed alternative schemes of greater and lesser ambition, but none were implemented.

On 5 October 1910, the Portuguese Republican Party staged a coup d'état that deposed the Portuguese monarchy and then began to implement policies for the modernization of Portugal's colonies. This eventually led to the establishment of the Missão de Melhoramento do Porto de Macau (Office for the Improvement of Macau's Harbor) in 1919, with Portuguese engineer Hugo Carvalho de Lacerda in charge. Lacerda was a visionary who devised and published a series of proposals for vast reclamations around Macau, most of which were unrealized.[6] His first significant work was the creation of Patane Port adjacent to Ilha Verde, a small island in the Porto Interior that was originally located about a kilometer offshore, then connected in 1895 to the peninsula by a causeway and subsequently engulfed by incremental land reclamation. He attempted to create new residential areas on either side of the northern isthmus, leading to confrontations with the Chinese residents over the location of the territorial border, which hadn't been precisely defined in the 1887 treaty.

To avoid further trouble, and simultaneously make a concerted attempt to catch up with Hong Kong's accelerating economy, Lacerda decided to abandon the Porto Interior and initiate a hugely ambitious project to create a Porto Exterior (Outer Harbor) at the northeast side of the peninsula facing onto the Pearl River Delta. Work began in 1923, undertaken by the Netherlands Harbour Works Company, and the new seaport was provisionally opened a few years later.[7] The Porto Exterior never became a significant international trading hub, initially serving only Chinese fishing boats and the occasional steamship from Lisbon. It is now used mainly by ferries to and from Hong Kong and other cities in the Pearl River Delta.

The most substantial legacy of Lacerda's work came from a side effect: 5 million cubic meters of sludge were dredged from the seabed and transformed into 125 hectares of new land.[8] Most of it was used to straighten and widen the eastern seaboard of Macau, creating a 1.5-kilometer stretch of new ground known as ZAPE (Zona Aterros do Porto Exterior). Lacerda produced a master plan for ZAPE in the 1920s, which comprised a street grid defining large plots, but it was never implemented. A terminal and pier were built for Pan American World Airways "flying boats" in the mid-1930s, but this only required a tiny fraction of the available area.

Left: Dennis Lau, Grand Lisboa Hotel and Casino, 2007.

Courtesy Dennis Lau & Ng Chun Man Architects and Engineers

Below: Gary Goddard, Galaxy Macau, 2011.

Courtesy Galaxy Entertainment Group

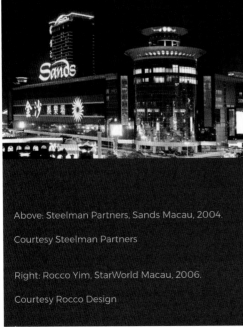

Above: Steelman Partners, Sands Macau, 2004.

Courtesy Steelman Partners

Right: Rocco Yim, StarWorld Macau, 2006.

Courtesy Rocco Design

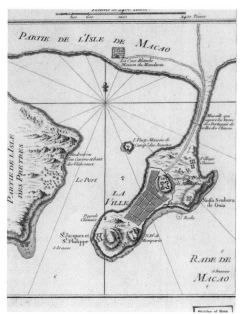

"Plan de la Ville et du Port de Macao," from Jacques Nicolas Bellin, *Le Petit Atlas Maritime, Tome III, No. 57* (Paris, 1764).

Planta da Peninsula de Macau (Lisbona: Sociedade de Geographia de Lisboa, 1889).

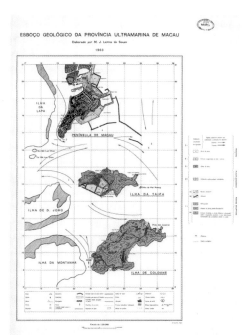

Esboço Geológico da Província Ultramarina de Macau (Macau: Imprensa Nacional de Macau, 1963)

Aerial view of the Macau peninsula in 1941. Courtesy DSSOPT.

"Peninsula de Macau e Ilha da Taipa contendo a planta das obras dos portos," from Hugo de Lacerda, Obras dos Portos de Macau: Memórias e Principais Documentos desde 1924 (Macau: Direcção das Obras dos Portos, 1925).

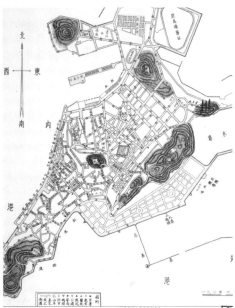

"City Plan of Macau (Ao-men)", from Commercial and Industrial Yearbook 1952-53 (Macau: Governo de Macau, 1953).

Aerial view of the Macau peninsula in 1988. Courtesy DSSOPT.

Aerial view of the Macau peninsula in 1998. Courtesy DSSOPT.

ZAPE in the 1980s,
(Macau archives).

Territorio de Macau, 1991.

(Macau: Direcção dos Serviços de Cartografia e Cadastro, 1991).

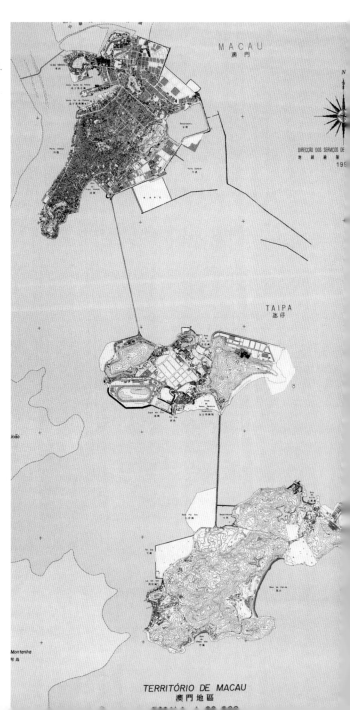

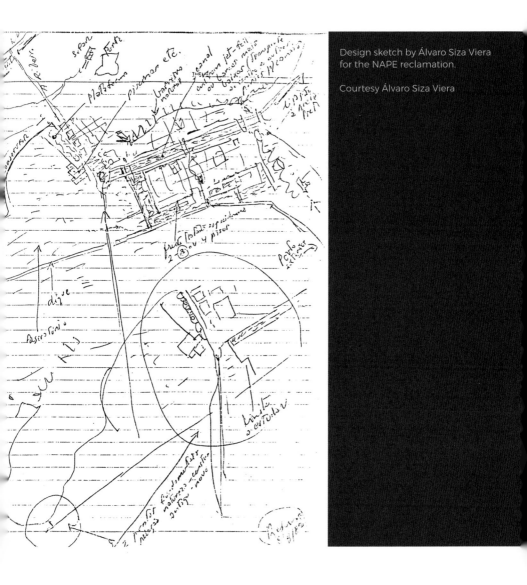

Design sketch by Álvaro Siza Viera for the NAPE reclamation.

Courtesy Álvaro Siza Viera

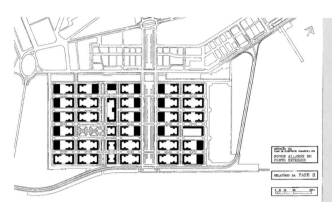

REVISÃO DO
PLANO DE EXISTÊNCIA URBANÍSTICA DOS
NOVOS ATERROS DO
PORTO EXTERIOR

RELATÓRIO DA FASE II

A MORFOLOGIA URBANA

Left: Official NAPE planning regulations published by the Macau government in 1991.

Below: NAPE view to east, 1998.

During the World War II, ZAPE was the site of temporary shelters for refugees from the Japanese occupation of Hong Kong and Shanghai.[9] Initially, Japan accepted that Portuguese neutrality also applied to Macau, but in 1943 Japanese troops crossed the border from China into Macau, resulting in firefights and fatalities, following which Japanese advisors were installed in the Macau government for the remainder of the war. The U.S. suspected that the Japanese military was attempting to procure fuel and other supplies in Macau, leading to the bombing of warehouses in ZAPE in January 1945. Though postwar tourist maps seem to show ZAPE covered with streets and building lots, contemporaneous photos reveal that the area stayed largely undeveloped right up until the 1980s, appropriated by mainland Chinese immigrants for growing vegetables.

The gaming industry had taken off in 1930, the year that a monopoly on casino-style games of chance was granted to the Hou Heng Company, which quickly opened a casino inside the Central Hotel. Compared to the seedy fantan houses and street stalls that previously dominated the industry, Hou Heng created luxurious interiors for their gaming rooms, offering customers free snacks, cigarettes, entertainment, and ferry tickets. Other types of gambling—primarily horse and dog racing—were then consolidated into a new monopoly granted to the Tai Heng Company in 1937, which became even more lucrative when mainland China outlawed gambling in 1949.

The Tai Heng monopoly expired in 1961, which was also the year that then-Governor Jaime Silvério Marques designated Macau a "permanent gaming region" with gaming-based tourism at the heart of the economy. A new gaming monopoly concession was opened to public bids, but only two companies applied: Tai Heng and STDM (Sociedade de Turismo e Diversões de Macau). The latter was a partnership led by Hong Kong-born entrepreneur Stanley Ho, who had made his fortune in the Macau black market during the World War II. STDM won the monopoly license, largely due to their promise to promote tourism by building many new casinos and hotels in ZAPE. They immediately turned a large Chinese junk into a floating casino, and opened the Casino Estoril in the city center. In 1963, Portuguese architects Leopoldo de Almeida and Manuel Vicente were asked to produce a new master plan for the ZAPE reclamation,[10] and STDM followed their proposed street layout, building the famed Lisboa Hotel and Casino at the southern tip of ZAPE.

Completed in 1970, the Lisboa was the first of Macau's casinos to be built on reclaimed land and one of the few buildings to follow Almeida and Vicente's ZAPE master plan.[11] The rest of the area saw only minor, haphazard development until 1979, when Jon Prescott (a British-born, Hong Kong-based architect) and Eduardo Lima Soares (Prescott's Macau branch office director) created yet another master plan for the area. It comprised a new street layout and lot divisions, areas designated for public facilities including a park, along with guidelines for building functions and morphology (primarily commercial podiums supporting residential slabs).[12] Again, almost none of this was implemented.

In 1981, the government finally established an urban planning division called the DSSOPT (Direcção dos Serviços de Solos, Obras Públicas e Transporte), led by newly arrived Portuguese architect Carlos Macedo e Couto. At his request, the ZAPE plan was revised by Prescott's employees Eduardo José Vicente Flores, who had replaced Lima Soares as Prescott's Macau office director, and American architect Peter Sydell. Flores added a network of pedestrian alleyways and arcaded sidewalks along the streets, along with a detailed landscaping design.[13]

In order to maintain the total floor area required by the government, the maximum allowable height was raised from 60 meters to 90 meters in one part of ZAPE, while being lowered elsewhere so as to preserve sightlines to the seventeenth-century fortress on Guia Hill. After requesting sundry other changes, which resulted in many of Flores's picturesquely angled streets being straightened, the government publicly announced the ZAPE master plan guidelines. However, these were never legally enforced, so building permits could still be issued for designs that didn't comply.[14] The cumulative result was a cluster of casino-hotels near the Lisboa, and a general sense of visual and formal incoherence elsewhere. By this time, the vegetable gardens had mostly vanished and some residential buildings had appeared, but many ZAPE sites would remain empty or half built until the 1990s.

During his eight-year tenure as head of the DSSOPT, Couto assembled a small group of architects to oversee new planning projects

Eduardo Lima Soares, model
of original urban plan for Cotai.

Courtesy estate of
Eduardo Lima Soares.

Original model of the Las
Vegas Sands Corporation plan
for the Cotai Strip, 2002.

Courtesy Las Vegas
Sands Corporation

in Macau. Rather than try to impose an overall master plan on the incoherent city he had inherited, Couto commissioned outside offices to produce designs for various districts, while his own team worked on solving the connections between them. The largest initiatives were two huge reclamation projects on the eastern side of the peninsula: Novos Aterros da Areia Preta, and NAPE (Novos Aterros do Porto Exterior). NAPE was a 110-hectare area that was to extend into the sea immediately adjacent to ZAPE. An invited competition was held in 1984, and won by Hong Kong's Palmer & Turner Group leading an international team (Euroconsult, Deloitte Haskins & Sells, Maunsell Consultants Asia, Collier Petty Chartered Surveyors, Gabinete de Estudos Técnicos), with Portuguese architect Álvaro Siza retained as a design consultant.[15]

Whereas ZAPE was an irregular, distorted strip contiguous with the existing coastline, NAPE was intended to be a clean break figuratively and literally: a semi-autonomous district separated from the ZAPE waterfront by a canal, laid out with simple geometric clarity in deliberate contrast to the ad hoc organicism and contingency of urban planning elsewhere in Macau. Siza's initial proposal was influenced by the nineteenth-century Cerdà plan[16] for Barcelona and took its module from the typical planning of Spanish colonial cities: a 144 x 144-meter grid of streets defining relatively low blocks with central courtyards. He used exactly those dimensions in the residential development designed for Areia Preta, but at NAPE the module was split in half to create a rectangular street grid, bisected by a linear park that formed an extension of the ZAPE park.

The NAPE master plan was enforced by law, with a special body established by the DSSOPT to administer its execution and detailed regulations laid out in a 175-page document published by the government.[17] These specify a block morphology of commercial podiums supporting mid-rise perimeter slabs, thus defining central courtyard spaces, along with floor-area ratios, lot coverages, and building heights. Nonetheless, commercial concerns led the government to increase the maximum building height set by Siza from 22 meters to 80 meters.[18] Reclamation began in 1988, and the first buildings were completed in the mid-1990s, but some plots remain vacant two decades later.

Though Couto and the DSSOPT did finally produce a master plan for Macau in 1987, the relatively autonomous planning of individual districts over the preceding few years—not to mention centuries of haphazard, permissive growth—has profoundly affected contemporary urban conditions. Macau's urban identity displays a kind of cognitive dissonance that compels each new development to attempt to restore a degree of balance to the accumulating incongruities of the past. The result is an exhilarating and sometimes disturbing sense of disorientation, which has only increased since Portuguese control ended and the gaming industry has become increasingly dominant in each successive expansion of the territory.

In the period leading up to the handover, the Beijing government decided that Macau could keep on building casinos but no Chinese money could be invested in them. In response, the local government declined to renew STDM's monopoly of STDM when it expired in 2002. STDM now operates its casinos through a subsidiary called SJM (Sociedade de Jogos de Macau). The opportunity to bid for gaming concessions was offered to international casino corporations, which immediately descended on the large open plots remaining in the NAPE area.[19]

In 2004, the Las Vegas Sands Corporation opened Macau's first foreign-owned casino. Located at the east edge of NAPE, it blocks most of a site that had been reserved for a vast waterfront park. Other violations of the regulations followed, with the government selectively repealing aspects of the official master plan. Though already built, the streets on the west side of NAPE were reorganized to create two massive lots for the Wynn and MGM Grand casinos. Completed in 2006 and 2007, respectively, each has a footprint, height, form, and image that completely contravene the NAPE master plan.

The canal dividing ZAPE and NAPE suffered from silting and mosquito infestation, so it was refilled and turned into a public park called Jardim das Artes, next to which is the StarWorld casino, a thirty-nine-story agglomeration of glass-clad boxes designed by Hong Kong architect Rocco Yim and completed in 2006. It projects over Avenida da Amizade (the former waterfront road), diverting traffic flow in order to create a private drop-off zone for casino buses and taxis. Far higher than the allowable height limit for NAPE, the StarWorld was at the time the tallest building

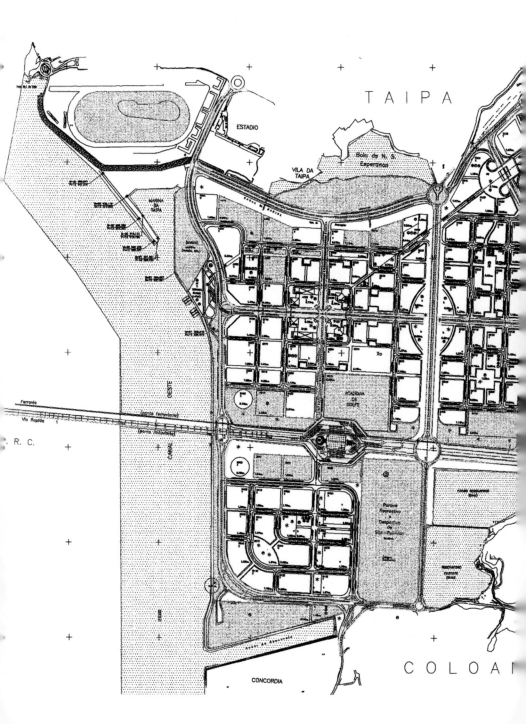

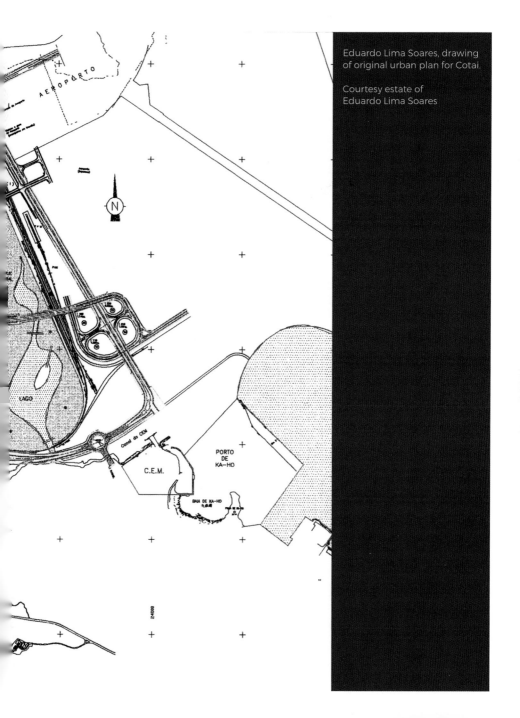

Eduardo Lima Soares, drawing of original urban plan for Cotai.

Courtesy estate of Eduardo Lima Soares

AEDES, Sands Cotai Central, 2012.

Courtesy Las Vegas Sands Corporation

The Cotai Strip by night.

Photo: Luís Almoster

The Cotai Strip as seen from Coloane.

Photo: Luís Almoster

in Macau. A local resident sued the government for illegally issuing the building permit. In response, the government publicly described the NAPE master plan as outdated and impractical, then in 2007 repealed it entirely. Nonetheless, it was such flagrant violations of the law, and the concomitant bribery, that contributed to Ao Man Long (the SAR's first Secretary for Transport and Public Works) being arrested in 2006 and in 2008 sentenced to almost three decades in prison.

Besides the new international airport, built out into the sea east of Taipa, the other major land reclamation development initiated prior to the handover is the area now known as Cotai, a portmanteau name coined to describe the 6 square kilometers of new territory between Coloane and Taipa, which turned the two islands into a single, 20-square-kilometer landmass. It is here that the use of reclaimed land as a blank slate for developments of unprecedented scale and splendor reaches its apotheosis.

The idea of completely filling the areas of open sea in Macau dates at least to the early twentieth century. In 1918, a group of Canadian engineers made a proposal to reclaim the area between the islands, and in 1927 the Portuguese administration published a scheme that would transform the peninsula and islands into a single piece of land. Coloane and Taipa were first physically connected in 1969 by a 2-kilometer-long causeway called the Estrada do Istmo (Isthmus Road). Having decided to reclaim the area between the islands, DSSOPT held a design competition in 1992 for what was officially titled Nova Cidade de Cotai, a new town intended for 150,000 residents and 80,000 nonresident workers.[20] The winning architect, Eduardo Lima Soares (assisted by Jon Prescott and Mário Neves), produced an urban plan predominantly comprising housing and ancillary social facilities—health, education, recreation—with generous allotments of greenery and water reservoirs. Smaller areas were allocated for tourism activities, mostly on the west side, facing Hengqin Island and physically connected to it by the new Lotus Bridge.[21]

Reclamation on the west side of the Estrada do Istmo began in the late 1990s. António José Castanheira Lourenço, head of GADA (Gabinete para o Apoio ao Desenvolvimento dos Aterros Taipa-Coloane, the government department in charge of developing Cotai) stated in 1998,

> The new city is designed to help with the enclave's future economic and population growth and provide a good quality of life by equipping it with social installations for sports, culture, education, health, and leisure activities.... In order to achieve these goals, high standards were set to keep the population density low on the urbanization scale.[22]

Fine ambitions to be sure, but realizing them entailed finding corporations willing to build housing developments on the individual sites. Uncertainty over Macau's future under Chinese rule, combined with the 1997 Asian financial crisis, made potential investors wary. GADA eventually (and somewhat desperately) sold the Cotai sites to casino developers at prices that have never been made public but are generally assumed to have been absurdly low.[23]

It wasn't necessary to make radical changes to Lima Soares's urban design. GADA simply erased some of the planned secondary roads in order to create larger lots. The main investor was the Las Vegas Sands Corporation. In an epiphany similar to Bugsy Siegel's vision of a gambling mecca in the empty Nevada desert, Sands CEO Sheldon Adelson visited the swampy surroundings of the former Estrada do Istmo in 2002 and reconceived it as the Cotai Strip—a magnificent avenue lined with luxury hotels and casinos, many owned by other corporations but all within his master plan.

The SARS (severe acute respiratory syndrome) outbreak from 2002 to 2003 slowed all development in Macau and Hong Kong, temporarily causing a huge drop in property prices that international casino corporations were quick to exploit. Having assembled the necessary investors, Adelson officiated at the groundbreaking ceremony for the Cotai Strip on 1 March 2007, and the Venetian Macao (the largest casino in the world) opened for business in August that year.

Development was again brought to a virtual standstill in 2008 by the combined effect of the global financial crisis and a governmental decision suspending the issue of new gaming concessions and banning casinos on any future land reclamations. The Las Vegas Sands Corporation came close to bankruptcy, but soon recovered. By 2012, the remaining development applications had been approved.[24] Since then,

Overview of the Novas
Zonas Urbanas proposal.
Courtesy DSSOPT

five of the six casino operators active in Macau (Las Vegas Sands, MGM, Wynn Resorts, Galaxy Entertainment Group, Melco Crown, but not SJM) have opened multiple casinos in Cotai.

So far, there are no housing developments in Cotai proper, merely a few luxury apartment complexes around the periphery. The intended residents of Cotai have presumably settled in the Macau peninsula, Taipa, or Coloane. As property prices continue to be pushed up by the lack of space and the huge profits generated by gaming, many Macau citizens choose to live in China, commuting across the border each day.

Clearly, venality has compromised most of these attempts to relieve congestion in Macau's old residential neighborhoods and keep pace with immigration-fueled population growth. If the Macau Special Administrative Region was conceived by Beijing as a social pressure valve for China—a quarantined zone intended to entice and exhaust vice while preventing the wider contamination of respectable Chinese society— it is precisely this containment that forces its constant physical expansion. However, one consequence of the handover was Macau's loss of its territorial waters: the surrounding sea was put under Chinese jurisdiction, with any new land reclamation requiring approval from Beijing.[25]

In 2006, Macau initiated plans to add another seven square kilometers around the east and south of the peninsula and the north of Taipa, to be collectively known as the Novas Zonas Urbanas (New Urban Zones). Beijing finally gave permission in 2009 but for only half that surface area, stipulating that the new areas should contain varying proportions of residential, commercial, industrial, recreational, institutional, and infrastructural facilities but no gaming facilities of any kind. Two alternative schemes— the differences are relatively minor variations of density and program—were produced by CAUPD (China Academy of Urban Planning and Design), and huge, beguiling models and renderings were placed on display at the Macau Science Center from late 2011 to early 2012.[26]

The three-and-a-half square kilometer area of the Novas Zonas Urbanas is divided into five districts: two are localized extensions into the sea, and three are small islands that will preserve the profile of the existing coastline and create semi-sheltered bays. The majority of

Macau's existing planning regulations have been provisionally suspended, on the assumption that a new planning code will emerge in parallel with the development of the design—an audacious decision that risks being exploited but is optimistically aimed at the generation of productive new urban paradigms appropriate to local cultural and climatic conditions.

While this seems to entail a provisional halt to the growth of Macau's gaming industry, other outlets are being found for the investment and development energy that has been repressed. On Hengqin Island, now part of the Zhuhai Special Economic Zone, the Macau SAR government has leased 1.1 square kilometers of reclaimed land for the University of Macau's new campus (designed by architect He Jingtang, best known for the China pavilion at the 2010 Shanghai Expo), accessed from Cotai by an underwater tunnel without going through immigration or customs.

The lease will expire at the same moment as the SAR status, but in the meantime the campus is under liberal Macau's jurisdiction: a West Berlin–like moated enclave, an oasis of capitalism surrounded by communism. While a university campus may be innocent enough, since 2005 the Las Vegas Sands Corporation has been negotiating with the Zhuhai government to build a leisure and convention resort more than five square kilometers in area, incorporating hotels, convention facilities, golf courses, marinas, and so on. Gaming would remain illegal, but for Sheldon Adelson, these facilities would be a complementary annex to Cotai. In the original 2005 press release he asserted, "The strategic combination of noncasino tourism amenities located on Hengqin Island with the entertainment attractions of the Cotai Strip could create a tourism and convention destination unrivaled anywhere in the world."[27] The Las Vegas Sands Corporation has also proposed that this development receive the same legal status as the University of Macau campus, potentially expanding the area available for Macau-style integrated resorts across the rest of Hengqin Island's 96 square kilometers.

As Macau continues to expand into the sea, encroach on Chinese territory, and merge into a single, physically continuous landmass, it is becoming an accumulation of distinct urban environments with contrasting degrees of density, permeability, interiority, illumination, color, and atmosphere. It is a collage city, a mosaic of contiguous yet discrete Macaus that manifest changes in circumstance and ideology over five centuries. The juxtaposition of radically incommensurable city fragments may be clear enough from above, but experientially one always seems to be immersed in a consistent condition, whether the baroque colonial city, the labyrinthine Chinese neighborhoods, the predominantly Filipino quarters, the waterfront industrial heritage, the tourist-oriented historical villages, the master-planned grids of commercial and residential blocks, the semiautonomous luxury housing developments, the casino precincts, or the integrated resorts themselves. Rather than the new overwhelming the old, or enhancing it by contrast, the surviving traditional districts are on the verge of becoming just another part of the patchwork, no more and no less authentic or primordial than any other.

Macau today provides a case study of the implications and potentials for piecemeal tabula rasa planning: not a palimpsest of historical layers within a contained territory but a proliferation of adjacent alternatives, an array of experimental results left permanently on display.

Acknowledgments

I would like to thank architects Carlos Couto, Eduardo Flores, Francisco Vizeu Pinheiro, Nuno Soares, and the staff of the Arquivo Histórico de Macau for assistance in researching this essay.

Notes

1. António de Oliveira Salazar, Discurso sobre o ultramar na Assembleia Nacional, June 1961, quoted in Francisco Gonçalves Pereira, Portugal, a China e a "Questão de Macau" (Macau: Instituto Português do Oriente, 1995). English translation taken from Trigo de Sousa, Regional Integration and Differentiation in a Globalizing China: The Blending of Government and Business in Post-Colonial Macau (Amsterdam: Institute for Social Science Research, 2009).

2. Victor F. S. Sit, Macau through 500 Years: Emergence and Development of an Untypical Chinese City (Hong Kong: Enrich Professional Publishing, 2012).

3. Armando Azenha Cação, "San Kiu," Review of Culture, no.36–37 (2nd series 1998):199–215.

4. Lindsay Ride and May Ride, *The Voices of Macao Stones* (Hong Kong: Hong Kong University Press, 1999), 44–49.

5. C. A. Montalto de Jesus, *Historic Macao* (Oxford: Oxford University Press, 1926), 430.

6. Hugo de Lacerda, *Macau e seu futuro porto* (Macau: N. T. Fernandes e Filhos, 1922), and Obras dos portos de Macau: *memorias e principais documentos* desde 1924 (Macau, N. T. Fernandes e Filhos, 1925). See also Macau *e seu porto artificial: atravez a imprensa Portuguesa* (Macau: Tipografia Mercantil, 1924).

7. Hugo de Lacerda, *Apontamentos gerais sobre as obras dos portos de Macau* (Macau: Direcção das Obras dos Portos, 1927).

8. Manuel Teixeira and C. R. Boxer, *Marinheiros ilustres relacionados com Macau* (Macau: Centro de Estudos Maritimos de Macau, 1988).

9. Peter Haberzettl and Roderich Ptak, "Macao and Its Harbour: Projects Planned and Projects Realized (1883–1927)," *Bulletin de l'École française d'Extrême-Orient* 78(1991):297–316.

10. Leopoldo de Almeida, "Notas de uma viagem a Macau," *Arquitectura-Lisboa* 84(November 1964):131–37.

11. Maria de Lourdes Rodrigues Costa, *História da arquitectura em Macau* (Macau: Cultural Institute of Macau, 1997).

12. Jon A. Prescott, *Macaensis Momentum: A Fragment of Architecture, a Moment in the History of the Development of Macau* (Macau: Hewell Publications, 1993).

13. Mário Neves, "Entrevista com Jon Prescott," *Arquitectura: Revista da Associação dos Arquitectos de Macau* 4 (July/August 1992):30–35.

14. Bruce Taylor, "Planning for High Concentration Development: Reclamation Areas in Macau," in *Population and Development in Macau*, ed. Rufino Ramos et al. (Macau: University of Macau, 1994).

15. Matt Davies, ed., *P & T Group: 140 Years of Architecture in Asia* (Mulgrave, AU: Images Publishing, 2008).

16. Álvaro Siza, *Immaginare l'evidenza* (Bari: Editori Laterza, 1998).

17. Governo de Macau, *Boletim Oficial de Macau*, 2.º Suplemento, no. 15 (18 April 1991).

18. Peter Testa and Peter Brinckhert, "Il piano di Macao: progetti di Álvaro Siza Viera," *Casabella* 559(1989):4–14.

19. Thomas Chung and Hendrik Tieben, eds., "Macao 1999–2009: Architecture and Urbanism in the First Post-Handover Decade," *World Architecture* 234:12 (2009), 18–129.

20. *COTAI: a nova cidade no território de Macau — futuros aterros inter-ilhas Taipa-Coloane* (Macau: Gabinete para Apoio ao Desenvolvimento dos Aterros Taipa-Coloane, 1999).

21. Agnes Lam Iok Fong, ed., *21st Century Macau City Planning Guideline Study 1999–2020* (Macau: Fundação para a Cooperação e o Desenvolvimento de Macau, 1999).

22. Quoted in Gilberto Lopes, "Projects for the 21st Century," *Macau* (1998), 7–17.

23. Penny Wan and Francisco Vizeu Pinheiro, "The Development of the Gaming Industry and Its Impact on Land Use," in *Gaming, Governance and Public Policy in Macao*, eds. Newman M. K. Lam and Ian Scott (Hong Kong: Hong Kong University Press, 2011), 19–35.

24. Emanuel Graça, "Full House," *Macau Business* (November 2012), 64–66.

25. In 2015, the Macau SAR was granted 85 square kilometers of territorial waters to the east and south of the peninsula, but Beijing's permission is still required for reclamation or infrastructure projects in this area.

26. "Anteprojeto do plano director das novas zonas urbanas: documento de consulta relative," (Macau: DSSOPT, 2011).

27. Las Vegas Sands Corporation press release, 17 October 2005.

MACAU LAND RECLAMATION 1912-2011

When the Portuguese arrived in the sixteenth century, Macau totaled only 2.78 km2. By the early twentieth century, it grew to 11km2. In 2015, Macau is 30km2, more than ten times its original size.

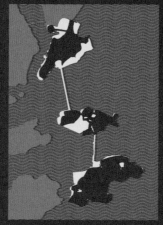

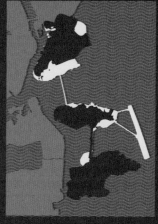

1912

Macau Peninsula 3.4 km²
Taipa 2.3 km²
Cotai 0 km²
Coloane 5.9 km²
Total area 11.6 km²

1986

Macau Peninsula 5.8 km² (+71%)
Taipa 3.7 km² (+61%)
Cotai 0 km²
Coloane 7.1 km² (+20%)
Total area 16.6 km² (+43%)

2000

Macau Peninsula 8.5 km² (+47%)
Taipa 6.2 km² (+68%)
Cotai 3.1 km²
Coloane 7.6 km² (+7%)
Total area 25.4 km² (+53%)

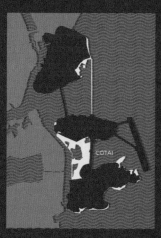

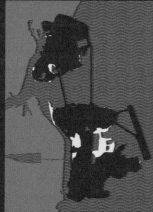

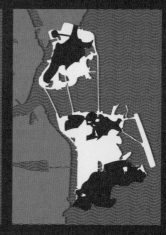

2004

Macau Peninsula 8.8 km² (+3%)
Taipa 6.4 km² (+3%)
Cotai 4.7 km² (+52%)
Coloane 7.6 km²
Total area 27.5 km² (+8%)

2011

Macau Peninsula 9.3 km² (+6%)
Taipa 7.4 km² (+16%)
Cotai 5.6 km² (+19%)
Coloane 7.6 km²
Total area 29.9 km² (+9%)

1912-2011

Macau Peninsula 9.3 km² (+174%)
Taipa 7.4 km² (+69%)
Cotai 5.6 km²
Coloane 7.6 km² (+22%)
Total area 29.9 km² (+158%)

DEVELOPMENT OF COTAI

In 1969, a two-kilometer-long causeway connected Coloane and Taipa islands. Since the 1990s, the area between the islands has been reclaimed to form Cotai, a portmanteau of Coloane and Taipa.

CHAPTER 3

SPECTACULAR ARCHITECTURE AT THE FRONTIERS OF GLOBAL CAPITALISM

TIM SIMPSON

To contemplate the new architecture dominating Macau's increasingly fantastical cityscape, consider first that Macau is a tiny enclave, comprised of only 30.3 square kilometers. With 600,000 residents, it is the most densely populated territory in the world. The huge numbers of additional tourists—31 million of them visited Macau in 2014 alone—exponentially increase the population density and scarcity of space.

There are more than 200,000 cars in this crowded city, making driving surprisingly tedious and stressful for what is an otherwise small, accessible, and seemingly convenient locale. The maximum speed limit in town is 60 kph (or 80 kph on the two longest bridges that connect the islands of Macau and Taipa) but there are exceedingly rare opportunities on the interior city roads to even reach that speed, much less sustain it for more than a few seconds. Central Macau's narrow, twisting streets resemble a byzantine medieval labyrinth more than a modern roadway system. Most driving therefore occurs on narrow and congested streets with frequent starts and stops, blockages, traffic jams, and the constant presence of large numbers of tourist pedestrians swarming across roads, often without regard for traffic signals or right-of-way.

Yet, even in the face of such an automobile-unfriendly environment, Macau registers an astounding number of high-octane, luxury sports cars, including (as of September 2014) 131 Ferraris, 106 Lamborghinis, and 158 Maseratis.[1] If one includes Macau's 523 Bentleys and 250 Rolls-Royces, there are approximately two such cars for every kilometer of road in the city. To put into perspective the incongruity of these muscular cars on Macau's diminutive streets, it would take less than three seconds for a new Ferrari Berlinetta to accelerate from a standstill to well beyond Macau's maximum speed limit, and it would be virtually impossible to find an unoccupied piece of straight pavement where this three-second drive would even be possible without careening into other cars or running down hapless pedestrians. Suffice it to say there are rare opportunities in Macau for the moneyed driver of a Ferrari or Lamborghini to take the car above second gear.

These incongruous, superlative automobiles on Macau's crowded roadways are an unintentional allegory for Macau's equally ostentatious contemporary architectural developments. The sleek purple Lamborghini clumsily navigating the narrow streets of a city for which it was clearly not designed mimics the construction in the tiny territory of imposing edifices such as the gargantuan Venetian Macao (its official spelling) and the glittering iconic glass tower of the Grand Lisboa. These buildings simply do not seem to fit.

Macau's Spectacular Cityscape

Purportedly 40 percent larger than the Pentagon, the Venetian Macao Integrated Resort is the largest building in Asia and the largest themed environment on the planet, yet it was constructed in one of the world's smallest sovereign territories. Built at a cost of $2.4 billion, the Venetian is an oversized copy of its counterpart, the Las Vegas Venetian, and a blatant act of plagiaristic appropriation of specific buildings, canals, monuments, and neighborhoods from the Italian city of Venice, complete with St. Mark's Square and the façade of Ducal Palace. The Venetian Macao features not only the world's largest casino but a 3000-room, all-suites hotel; a shopping mall with 350 retail shops (when it opened it was Macau's very first indoor shopping mall); a 15,000-seat auditorium offering NBA basketball games, professional tennis exhibitions, and concerts by Rihanna and Bon Jovi; three indoor canals plied by Filipino gondoliers; 1.2 million square feet of convention space; a large clinic offering an exclusive, patented form of dental reconstruction surgery; and the Adelson Advanced Education Center, an off-campus facility of the University of Macau. With residences, shopping, entertainment, a waterway, and even medical and educational facilities, the Venetian is a city unto itself. Indeed, the property is so spacious it would likely be easier to pilot a Ferrari through the interior of the gigantic structure than on the actual streets of Macau.

The Venetian, like the myriad Lamborghinis and Maseratis in Macau, is indicative of a tectonic shift in the global economy and a recomposition of capitalism away from the North American and Western European cities that dominated twentieth-century industry to the metropolitan environments of East Asia that already play such an important role in the twenty-first century. The city-state of Macau and its new casino complexes are crucial to the ongoing viability of global capitalism, because they are a conduit for the travels and tribulations of Chinese tourists, stops on what has become a contemporary Chinese version of the nineteenth-century European Grand Tour. Even though the Chinese economy is currently facing a downturn, the fact is that the viability of global capitalism, at least in the near term, will depend more and more on the deep pockets of Chinese consumers. Gambling and luxury shopping sites in Macau like the Venetian play a functional role in an inadvertent project that I call "consumer pedagogy": the didactic training of the post-socialist population of the People's Republic of China (PRC) to participate in the global consumer economy.[2]

The Shape of Macau's Economic Boom

The Venetian Macao is no anomaly. This structure joins the increasingly phantasmagoric post-colonial cityscape that has emerged in Macau since Portugal's handover of the territory to the PRC in 1999, and which now features a number of other themed resorts and five-star glass towers. These new structures contrast sharply with Macau's quaint, pastel-colored colonial-era Portuguese churches and municipal buildings that are now UNESCO World Heritage sites, as well as the shabby concrete apartment blocks and nondescript office buildings built in the last decades of the twentieth century. After liberalization of the casino industry in 2003, the new superlative structures rose rapidly in a profound transformation of Macau's built environment coupled with a massive influx of transnational capital. The break-up of the local casino monopoly held for forty years by Hong Kong billionaire Stanley Ho brought in gaming barons from Las Vegas, Australia, and Hong Kong, including Sheldon Adelson, Steve Wynn, James Packer, and Lui Che Woo. To date, these entrepreneurs have spent or are committed to almost $50 billion in new construction.

The Macau peninsula today features a collection of fantastical resorts. Adelson's golden glass Sands Casino, which opened in 2004, was the first foreign gaming foray into the territory. Built at a cost of $240 million, it quickly became the most profitable casino in the world, and Adelson recouped his initial investment within ten months of operation. The profits derived from Macau's gaming industry have been astonishing. By 2007, Adelson had become the third richest person in the United States. *Forbes* estimated that during the previous three years he earned $1 million per hour from his investments. However, Adelson faced stiff competition from other entrepreneurs in Macau whose properties sprang up almost as quickly in the same neighborhood. Steve Wynn constructed his eponymous Wynn Macau and Wynn Encore projects, with their tasteful brown glass curtain walls; Hong Kong property tycoon Liu Che Woo added the arresting Galaxy Star World, which features an illuminated surface of glass and light; the tricolored, undulating glass MGM Macau also features a reconstructed faux Portuguese palace and adjoining square under a glass atrium; and dominating the Macau skyline is the gigantic, lotus-shaped Grand Lisboa, local magnate Stanley Ho's answer to the competition

Incongruous muscle cars for Macau's diminuitive medieval streets. An unintenional allegory for the city's ostentatious architecture?

Photo: Tim Simpson

posed by these outgrowths of the Las Vegas style. Across the channel on Taipa Island, near Adelson's Venetian Macao on the Cotai Strip, sits Packer's City of Dreams, as well as the Sands Cotai, the Four Seasons, and the Galaxy Macau. Six new projects are currently under construction, including a $4 billion Wynn addition to Cotai; a Studio City structure with a figure-eight Ferris wheel, which will be the tallest in Asia, built into the building façade; and a Parisian Resort with a planned scale model of the Eiffel Tower.

Macau's Role in China's Economic Development

The money keeps pouring in, with 2013 gaming revenue of $45 billion. Both Macau's preponderance of luxury sports cars and the profits generated from the city's remarkable new casino resorts like the Venetian are products of the same phenomenon: the unprecedented growth of the mainland Chinese economy and rising levels of citizen wealth. This ongoing transformation is evident in the eager tourists queuing outside the Louis Vuitton, Hermès, and Chanel shops in Macau's resorts. Those purchases are no doubt fueled by the extraordinary rate at which new billionaires have been minted in the PRC, as well as across the Asia-Pacific region,

which as a whole has more wealthy residents than North America.[3] No doubt, some of these newly rich are driving Macau's Maseratis.

But the future of Chinese consumption will likely depend not on those millionaires and billionaires but on the members of the emerging middle class who increasingly visit Macau on tourist visas enabled by new central government policies. China manages economic growth by categorizing its provinces based on levels of affluence, selectively providing specific advantages to certain population segments. Such policies direct relatively affluent Chinese nationals toward consumer holidays in Macau. The central government's Individual Visa Scheme (IVS) allows select Chinese to travel to the Special Administrative Regions (SAR) of Macau and Hong Kong as individuals rather than as part of a government-sanctioned tour group. Therefore, these tourists' newfound freedom is a product of specific governmental calculation.

For its part, the central government continues to focus macroeconomic policy on encouraging Chinese consumers to spend their newfound wealth to drive the domestic economy. Such policies stand in stark contrast to the frugal, anticonsumption propaganda of the former socialist state. The implementation in 2000

The Venetian
Macao constitutes
an interiorized
city unto itself.

Photo: Ming-yen
Hsu, Flickr

of semiannual Golden Week holidays was a bold attempt to encourage domestic tourism. Proconsumption messages are more ubiquitous each year. For example, an editorial headline in *China Daily* in 2008 urged the government to "unleash consumption" to stimulate the economy. Macau plays a functional role in this effort.[4]

From my vantage point, living in Macau for more than a decade, it appears that the glass resorts and themed environments are indeed a crucial component of consumer pedagogy. Macau today appears not so much as a conventional city as it does a laboratory of consumption, a giant petri dish where a volatile cocktail of potent architectural products, liquid capital, baccarat tables, electronic slot machines, central govern-ment visa policies, and eager tourists are stirred in an alchemical effort to generate enormous economic returns. Tourists then take the ped-agogy of consumption back to the mainland.

Special Administrative Regions and Special Economic Zones

Understood in this way, we can see that the casino complexes in the Macau SAR operate in tandem with the factories in the Special

Economic Zones (SEZ) of Zhuhai and Shenzhen, just across the Chinese border. The SEZs were established as part of the opening up of the PRC to the global economic system that began in 1976 and the establishment of an indigenous market-socialist economy, or "socialism with Chinese characteristics." The SEZs attract vast sums of foreign investment and function "as social and economic laboratories where foreign technologies and managerial skills [can] be observed."[5] The pedagogical role of the SEZs is purposeful. Indeed, the Communist Party's own Science and Technology Modernization Imperative dictates, "The Shenzhen SEZ was deemed to be a 'learning laboratory of capitalist modes of operating business, high-tech manufacturing, and construction.'"[6] When he inaugurated Shenzhen in 1980, Chinese Premier Deng Xiaopeng was forthright in his hope that the SEZs would constitute a capitalist classroom.

> Special Economic Zones are a window to technology, management, knowledge, and foreign policies. Through the zones, we can import technology, acquire knowledge, and learn about management, which is also a form of knowledge. The Special Economic Zones will become a foundation for opening to the outside world.[7]

Understood as a laboratory for studying technology, management techniques, construction, and real estate, the didactic role of the SEZs is clear.

Macau as a Laboratory of Consumption

To "unleash" consumption implies a pent-up energy, primed to explode. However, consumption is not an inevitable process that will unfold naturally if permitted: it must be didactically encouraged and directed. Both the disciplining of the individual consuming subject and the management of the larger population toward consumer ends are elements of what Michel Foucault has called "bio-power," the calculation and mobilization of the very life of a nation's population towards specific economic goals. "This bio-power was without question an indispensable element in the development of capitalism," writes Foucault. "The latter would not have been possible without the controlled insertion of bodies into the machinery of production and the adjusting of the phenomenon of population to economic processes."[8] China's current economic reforms require a complementary "insertion of bodies" into the processes of consumption, and Macau's new casino resorts are sites where this process occurs, as tourists gather around a baccarat table or window shop in a resort.

Consumption involves not just a subjective desire for fashionable products. Consumption is a material practice that requires integration of that subject into material spaces designed and engineered for such a purpose. For this reason, arcades, department stores, fast-food outlets, and shopping malls have been crucial components in the historical development of capitalism. A contemporary architectural incarnation of these catalytic sites of consumption comes in the form of Macau's casino resorts.

Attention to the architecture of consumption in Macau reveals how the material environment enables behaviors and practices that contribute to an emergent post-socialist consumerist form of life, poised between the authoritarian political structure of the PRC and gradual increases in individual liberties that are part of the implementation of a market economy. The consumer spaces of Macau are of particular importance to understanding the increased movements of tourists today. The work of

consumerism is subject to the pedagogy of the market and the state, codified in material environments that serve a functional purpose.

Macau's Iconic Architecture

For Maria Kaika, Professor of Urban, Regional and Environmental Planning at the University of Amsterdam, the iconic buildings of the sort that characterize twenty-first-century Macau constitute a new category of architecture.[9] This architectural style is markedly different from the modernist structures built by moguls and philanthropists like Rockefeller or Carnegie that expressed twentieth-century industrial capitalism in cities in Europe and America. The visual experience of those cities was defined by the architectural movement known as the International Style. Popularized by architects such as Le Corbusier and Mies van der Rohe, the International Style shunned architectural ornamentation and embellishment in an effort to create a sleek modernist aesthetic of glass, steel, and concrete and exposed the functional element of the materials in the design. The goal was the honest expression of the building's structure. The corporate skyscraper became the iconic element of a modern cityscape, testament to the egos of the industrialists who funded their construction and their commitment to the social and cultural life of a particular city. Structures like Rockefeller Center not only served as the headquarters of enterprise but engaged the surrounding city, functioned in social ritual, enhanced public space, and contributed to civic life.[10]

Kaika contends that superlative architecture today, by contrast, illustrates a different type of iconicity. Structures such as Norman Foster's striking Swiss Re in London are primarily prestige products, initiated by companies whose operations are located elsewhere, funded by transnational elites with no particular local commitment, and designed by a celebrity starchitect whose name carries a marketable prestige factor. In Kaika's view, such buildings play no discernible role in the city in which they are located. Instead, they are temporary "totem[s] for flexible capitalism," built to impress tourists, not to serve the locals.[11] If the International Style sought the honest expression of structure, Macau's baroque resorts purposefully dissimulate, as glass, steel, and concrete masquerade as Himalayan mountain

Macau's loquacious architecture:
Grand Lisboa Hotel and Casino,
featuring the world's largest
integrated LED screen.

Photo: Tim Simpson

kingdoms and Renaissance marble palaces. Kaika characterizes this new type of architecture as "autistic"—architecture that does not dialogue with the surrounding city. It is uncommunicative architecture that serves only as a narcissistic display of corporate economic performance.

But although the buildings of Macau do indeed share some of these characteristics and may, no doubt, be seen as stark monuments to oversized entrepreneurial egos, it would not be entirely accurate to call these new resorts "autistic." In fact, whether or not we admire the aesthetic, Macau's iconic resorts do employ tens of thousands of locals, help maintain the negligible local unemployment rate of 2 percent, and contribute nearly 40 percent of gaming revenue in taxes. These monies fill government coffers and benefit the local population. Some of the funds are even returned directly to residents in the "wealth-sharing scheme" that began in 2008. In 2015, each permanent resident received a payment of MOP9000 ($1,100). Perhaps more importantly, the structures themselves play a fundamental role in not just captivating and bewitching tourists but a wholesale transformation of the Chinese population.

Far from being autistic, the "excessively narrated,"[12] themed environments of the Venetian Macao, Sands Cotai, and Fisherman's Wharf have an exuberance of signification, with a story seemingly bursting from every surface and fixture. Such themed environments feature overt architectural and design motifs that evoke associations with other cultures, times, or places. The narrative of the Venetian is further enhanced by "streetmospherics" that include living statues, opera singers, magicians, dancers, and other performers who appear among the simulated surfaces to entertain tourist visitors. The thematic narrative creates a commodified urban experience. That experience is part and parcel of the ongoing consumer pedagogy transforming the former communards of the PRC into the world's most dynamic consumers.

One might say, therefore, that Macau's new architecture is not so much autistic or uncommunicative as it is "loquacious".[13] These effusive buildings say too much; they offer an overabundance of signification. Like a bright yellow Ferrari or purple Lamborghini, Macau's verbose structures all but scream for attention. Today Macau's cityscape sparkles with all manner

of glass and crystalline amusements that participate in a pedagogical consumer project of world-historical significance. The football-shaped base of Ho's flagship Grand Lisboa Casino, which opened in 2007, is comprised of the world's largest integrated LED screen, featuring colorful displays of animated roulette wheels and rolling dice. The building's garrulous, mediated screen surface conjoins glass curtain construction, fiber optics technology, and images of gambling in an ideal representation of this new Chinese economic regime. Quite fittingly, displayed in the lobby of the casino is the world's largest cushion diamond, the $100 million, 218-carat Star of Stanley Ho. This symbolic apogee of gratuitous wealth seems somehow perfectly appropriate, set alongside the Lamborghinis and five-star ostentation so typical of tiny Macau's oversized contemporary cityscape.

Indeed, in terms of Macau's urban space, what is interesting is how these resorts are driving the development and expansion of the Macau territory itself. The entire Cotai area is comprised of reclaimed land that added 5.2 square kilometers to the territory. But in fact the resorts constructed on the Cotai Strip have actually increased the size of Macau's territory exponentially. The various hotel rooms, casinos, retail shops, and auditoriums of the Venetian and Sands-Cotai projects alone have collectively added 2.2 million square meters of space to Macau—which is to say they contribute nearly 8 percent in total interiorized space.[14]

A focus on the aesthetic form of these buildings, or the leisure activities they host, should not obscure their function as sites of tourist subjection. Their themed motifs and exaggerated surfaces provide the arena where post-socialist Chinese tourists engage in the kinesthetic work of becoming desiring adepts and practitioners of consumerism. They perfectly illustrate the role of spectacular architecture on a new frontier of global capitalism.

Notes

1. "Flash Cars almost Bumper-to-Bumper in Macau," *Macau Business Daily Newsletter*, 2 September 2015.

2. T. Simpson, "Materialist Pedagogy: The Function of Themed Environments in Post-Socialist Consumption in Macau," *Tourist*

MGM Macau:
spectacular architecture
at the frontiers of
global capitalism.

Photo: Tim Simpson

Studies 9, no. 1 (2009):60–80; T. Simpson,
"Neoliberalism with Chinese Characteristics:
Consumer Pedagogy in Macau," in *Cities
and Fascination: Beyond the Surplus of
Meaning*, H. Schmid, W. Sahr, and J. Urry,
eds., (Surrey, UK: Ashgate, 2011), 187–208.

3. "Soaring China Economy Mints New
Billionaires," *International Herald Tribune*,
14 October 2009, 4; S. Li, "More Super-
Rich in E. Asia than U.S.," *South China
Morning Post*, 29 March 2012, B1.

4. "Unleash Consumption," *China Daily*, 3 July
2006, 4.

5. D. Harvey, *A Brief History of Neoliberalism*
(Oxford: Oxford University Press, 2006), 130.

6. Chuihua Judy Chung, J. Inaba, R.
Koolhaas, and T. L. Sze, eds., *Great Leap
Forward* (Köln: Taschen, 2001), 121.

7. Quoted in Chiuhua et al., 2001:87.

8. M. Foucault, *The History of Sexuality*
(New York: Pantheon, 1978), 140–141.

9. M. Kaika, "Autistic Architecture: The Fall of
the Icon and the Rise of the Serial Object of
Architecture," *Environment and Planning
D: Society and Space* 29 (2011):968–992.

10. Ibid., p. 982.

11. Ibid., p. 976.

12. B. Lonsway, *Making Leisure Work:
Architecture and the Experience
Economy* (London: Routledge, 2009).

13. T. Simpson, 2014. "Macau Metropolis
and Mental Life: Interior Urbanism and the
Chinese Imaginary." *International Journal of
Urban and Regional Research* 38(3):823–842.

14. Ibid.

FREE SPECTACLE MAP

PONTE 16
Michael Jackson gallery: display of renowned on-stage costumes of the legendary king of pop, as well as his diamond gloves and videos of best-known performances.

GRAND LISBOA
Lavish exhibit of precious gems, diamonds, and crystals. Vast LED display at the exterior of the dome.

Crazy Paris Dance show (sexy dance shows including the French can can, India dance, and pole dancing) Show time: 2pm - 2am daily (one show per hour)

GRAND EMPEROR
'Changing of the Guard' ceremony: daily at hotel entrance.

Antique, 18th-century European golden carriage. 78 bars of pure gold at the Golden Pathway of the hotel lobby, each weighing 1kg.

LISBOA
Known for its Michelin-recommended fine dining restaurants, shopping arcade including jewelry stores, exhibited antiques and artworks, light-bulb-lined ceiling corridor, and large aquarium.

STARWORLD
Variety of live dance performances at the lobby. Daily rotating dance groups including Japanese divas, Korean pop, Brazilian dance and hip-hop, 1pm-6pm daily.

L' ARC
Victorian-style sauna; large pot of gold in the lobby.

MGM GRAND
Murano-glass ceiling sculptures; Salvador Dali sculpture.

Colonial-Portuguese architecture and a butterfly pavilion at the Grand Plaza.

PRESIDENT HOTEL
Portuguese colonial architectural elements.

WYNN
Tree of Prosperity: tree composed of 98,000 leaves of 24-karat gold and brass, rising underneath ceiling-dome with Chinese and western astrological symbols. Show time: every 30 minutes.

Performance lake: Dancing fountains with music, colored-light, and fire. Show time: every 30 minutes.

Moon Jellyfish Aquarium (at the lobby of the Encore Tower).

RIO
Furnished and designed as a royal Italian palace.

GOLDEN DRAGON
Sauna, nightclub. and billboard displays.

GRAND LAPA
Outdoor pool and high tea restaurant popular with Macau's Portuguese community.

SANDS
Live performers including the Baccarat Babes, Colombian All Stars, and the Sands Sirens.

CASINO BABYLON & FISHERMAN'S WHARF
A mixture of architectural heritage: Tudor homes, Roman Colosseum, and the Great Wall of China. Volcano rollercoaster and circus and street performers/clowns.

GALAXY
Fortune Diamond: water fountain with light and music. Show time: every 30 minutes.

Wishing Crystals: color-changing crystals pulsating with music. Every 30 minutes.

Galaxy Laserama: Laser show into Macau's night sky. Eight shows per night

ALTIRA
Thai massages and spa services. 16th-floor infinity pool with ocean view

Infographic by Alice Weng Sam Iu

NEW CENTURY
Greek and Roman mythology statues, sculptures, and water fountainsculptures & water fountain.

CITY OF DREAMS
Aquarium: mermaids swimming in a virtual underwater world. Show time: All-day.

Paid shows:
The House of Dancing Water: 2 shows per day.

Dragon's Treasure: 360-degree multimedia.

GRAND WALDO
Sauna and spa services.

FOUR SEASONS
Mediterranean Revival, Spanish Colonial Revival, and Moorish Revival architectural styles.

SANDS COTAI CENTRAL
Tibetan architectural elements.

VENETIAN MACAO
Magicians, singers and other "streetmosphere" performers;
Singing gondoliers at St. Mark's Square;
Latin dancers at Bar Florian;
Strings quartet and living statues at various floors.
Show time: all-day, every 15-30 minutes.

STUDIO CITY
Deep-space holographic projections at the food-court.

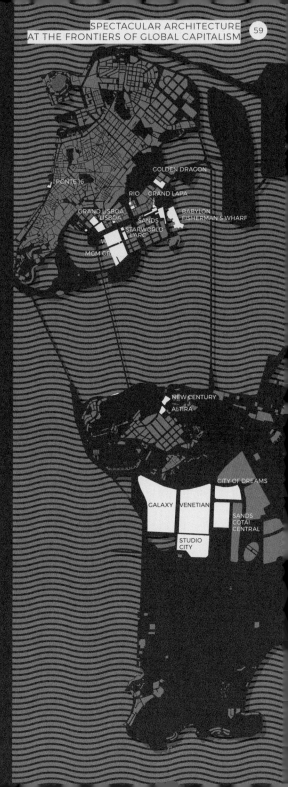

CHAPTER 4
HOTEL ESTORIL

TEXT AND IMAGES BY HK URBEX

A talented Italian architect produced the exquisite futurist mural on the hotel façade of this long-abandoned hotel. The forgotten structure now sits quietly on the edge of a prosperous neighborhood in the middle of Macau, rusting and decomposing, awaiting its fate. Yet this building is actually of great historical and cultural importance, for it played a key part in shaping the Macau we know today.

When the Hotel Estoril opened in 1963, it was the city's biggest casino, as well as Macau's first integrated gambling establishment, which established the paradigm on which the local gaming industry is now built. It was the first to excel at drawing in overseas tourists, offering luxury travel as well as gambling, adult entertainment, and everything in between. The brain behind it was none other than Stanley Ho, long before he became the casino mogul he is today.

The Hotel Estoril complex opened at a time when Macau was at a crossroads. The city had gone from a center for the opium trade to one focused on gold. As a maestro of the gold trade, Stanley Ho was well positioned for the next big thing in the enclave: gambling. Although gambling was nothing new in Macau, Ho took advantage of it in the best way possible and came to dominate the Macau gaming industry in a way only he could.

After winning the public tender for Macau's gaming monopoly, Ho set up Shun Tak Holdings to lure punters from Hong Kong via hydrofoils. He also brought in western game styles and promoted them to the Chinese, using Shanghai as his model. With his government-granted monopoly, he ruled

the Macau gaming industry for forty years and came to be known as the King of Gambling.

Hotel Estoril rapidly fell from grace, finally shutting its doors in the early 1990s. It has been left to rot ever since, and the beautiful Goddess of Fortune on its façade languishes. Inside are the gutted remains of what was once a heaving establishment: decaying hotel rooms, karaoke parlors, bar counters, music stages, and private baths. The dark, cavernous spaces within now hold an aura of fading mystery. On the ground floor are long rows of private bathing spaces and remnants of large sauna rooms, which would have been accessible only to a privileged few. Crumbling wall tiles and moldering furnishings reveal a scheme inspired by ancient Rome.

Most of the hotel rooms in the midmost areas of the hotel lie empty. Guestrooms that might once have held lavish parties have given way to new guests: nature and decay. Aside from vines, collapsing ceilings, and failing walls, there are skeletons of bed frames, altars to Chinese gods, and even a lonely piano in the corner of one pitch-black room.

Residual traces of former glory can be sensed on the upper floors of Hotel Estoril: one finds private lounges, suites, gaming rooms, and gambling halls. There is even a Princess Diana suite, which was probably a late addition. Windowless, the shadowy suite features large murals of the deceased Princess, resting in darkness. Although eerie, the murals are a solemn reminder of Diana's popularity at the time, a living symbol of wealth and royalty fit for a gambling palace.

Despite protest from preservationists and architects alike, the beautiful relic that is Hotel Estoril now faces the wrecking ball thanks to the government agenda. A Pritzker Prize-winning Portuguese architect favored by the authorities almost demolished the building to make way for an arts center and school, but the plan was later scrapped and the architect dropped from the project. Subsequently, Hotel Estoril was given a heritage evaluation in 2016, which apparently concluded the site had no cultural value.

Since then, there has been a lot of back and forth between government and preservationists, with one of the main areas of dispute being the exquisite futurist artwork on the façade. The masterpiece is part of the history of European presence in Macau. If demolished, Macau will lose another page from its history, and Hotel Estoril—with all its cultural significance—will disappear forever.

1. Many of the rooms have small shrines. This one contains a statue of Guan Yu, often worshipped as an alternative wealth god. 2. The extent of dilapidation is extreme, with some corridors looking more like ground zero. 3. Remains of the some of the lockers likely used by guests before entering the bathing areas. 4. This forlorn piano sits alone in a room, waiting for a pianist who will never return. 5. On the top of the hotel an old music stage and booths are all that remain of this restaurant. 6. The crumbling remains of Hotel Estoril serve as a solemn reminder of times gone by.

7. Classical touches can be seen on these metal window panels. 8. View from one of the private elevators reserved for distinguished guests. 9. On the ground floor are rows of private bathing spaces and the remains of large sauna rooms. 10. The Princess Diana suite. 11. On the ground floor are rows of private bathing spaces and the remains of large sauna rooms. 12. This open, mirrored area was likely for games and entertainment.

10

11

12

CHAPTER 5

CRITICAL REFLECTIONS ON THE MYTH OF THE CHINESE GAMBLER

KAH-WEE LEE

"In describing the vices of the Chinese, next to gambling must be considered opium smoking. The one is destructive to their moral and the other to their physical health."

— Sir Thomas Braddell, 1856 [1]

A nineteenth-century photograph taken in Hong Kong shows a group of Chinese gamblers gathered around a table to play a game of fantan. The setting suggests the interior of a house. In a game of fantan, the operator pulls out a random number of buttons or any other small articles, places them on the table, calls for bets, and then separates the buttons in batches of four. The remaining number of buttons in the last batch—1, 2, 3, or 4—is the winning number.

The stage of the game captured by this photograph is anything but innocent. The gamblers have already placed their bets on the table, and the operator has begun separating the buttons. What is presented is that moment when, as the number of buttons dwindles, the winning number becomes more and more apparent. It chooses to show that moment when all eyes are fixed to a single point on the table and other senses seem to shut down. The gamblers are so consumed by their concentration that every face is expressionless. The crooked shape of the gambler in the right foreground is perhaps the only suggestion of movement in this otherwise frozen tableau, but he does not lean onto the table as much as is propped up by it. To the left of the photograph, a man sitting behind a scale for weighing opium is drawn uncontrollably to the point of focus. The opium pipe carried by the crooked gambler, the ornate decoration of

the solid timber table, and the sunglasses worn by one of the gamblers—a western commodity and thus a signifier of luxury—complete the story of addiction with a subnarrative of indulgence. For a westerner like Sir Thomas Braddell, it is precisely this addiction and indulgence that is captured, communicated, and reinforced.

I have found this general structure of representation again and again in my research on the game of fantan and more generally in the history of the control of vice. From Canton to Macau to Singapore to Sydney to San Francisco to Nevada, the Orientalist gaze creates the figure of the "Chinese gambler" as inscrutable and self-explanatory, fascinating and repulsive. It is as if one image captures the raw essence of "Chineseness," a racial or civilizational constant that is impervious to modernity. It is as frozen as these gamblers are transfixed by a simple game of chance. The key elements of this timeless scene: the interiority of the setting, the centrality of the table, and the lifelessness of the ensorcelled gamblers.

Today, as Macau becomes the gateway to the largest gambling market in the world, the figure of the "Chinese gambler" has returned with a vengeance. The global casino industry is now the preeminent player in the quest to understand this mysterious figure. Gaming analysts observe

"Group of Chinese Gamblers," 1880s.
Source: National Archives of Singapore, Photo Accession No. 126044.

Chinese gamblers on the casino floor and distill their traits. Chinese gamblers are more "hardcore" than their Western counterparts, a report by an investment group says. Whereas westerners gamble with discretionary funds, Chinese gamblers use their savings, and the motivation is "driven by the need of getting financial stability that is deeply rooted in their civilization."[2] In professional journals, psychologists probe the cognitive patterns of the Chinese gambler: in contrast to their western counterparts, Chinese gamblers have a "strong illusion of control" and a heightened sense of risk-taking, which might explain their predilection for addiction.[3] In trade conferences like the G2E Asia, discussion panels are dedicated to decoding the consumption patterns of the "Chinese millennials" so as to court them better. Meanwhile, *feng shui* masters and casino designers warn of the innumerable taboos of Chinese cosmology while offering their services to tap into this new "science" of architectural and spatial design.

What is happening today is not simply a passive activity of understanding the Chinese gambler who exists somewhere out there, frozen in a timeless tableau. Rather, just as these images are far more eloquent about the prejudices

of the Orientalist gaze, such efforts should be recognized as attempts at *framing and producing* the ideal Chinese gambler. They reflect the moral-legal anxieties and commercial interests of the casino complex, defined loosely as a network of corporations, governments, professionals, and civic groups. To what extent can cultural habits be integrated into standard industry practices? How can popular games that Chinese gamblers like, such as baccarat, become more profitable? And conversely, how can Chinese gamblers be induced to play the more profitable but unpopular games such as slot machines? How can governments and corporations pursue their commercial interests within tolerable moral limits? In short, how can the responsible, law-abiding, and profitable Chinese gambler be produced and managed?

As many historians have shown, the control of vice through legalization always involves the active shaping of human subjectivity in order to conform to the dominant values of society. Indeed, before the modern casino and outside of the frozen image, gambling within the Chinese communities was more than what happened on the gambling table. It was part of social and economic life that stretched from the level of subsistence to that of

Dai Loy Gambling
House, Locke,
California

Source: Kah-
Wee Lee, 2012

geopolitics. To illustrate this rich tapestry, I will discuss two scenes— the Chinese migrant town of Locke in San Francisco in the 1920s and Macau in the late nineteenth-century —that are connected by a common ancestry in turn-of-the-century southern China. With these historical notes, I then return to the present and reflect critically on the current discourse about the Chinese gambler.

Locke, California, 1920s

Unlike other Chinatowns in the U.S., which were mostly enclaves within a larger white community, Locke began as an unincorporated township leased to Chinese migrant laborers in the 1920s in the Sacramento River Delta. In 1915, after the Chinatown in nearby Walnut Grove burned down, a group of workers from Zhongshan District—a province in Guangdong just north of Macau—leased land from the heirs of Mr. George Locke and began building this enclave.[4] Locke presents an interesting case that shows the self-organization of the Chinese community in a foreign land that discriminated against them. For the most part, there was little law enforcement by the Anglo-Americans, and the community policed itself.[5]

The first few buildings in the township were a saloon, boarding house, and gambling house. By 1920, there were restaurants, dry goods stores, hardware stores, a town hall and merchants' association hall, drug store, post office, theatre, flourmill, opium rooms, and brothels. The town was arranged along two main avenues— Main Street where most of the commercial activities could be found, and the secondary street parallel to it, Key Street, which was mainly residential. By 1930, there were three gambling houses along Main Street. Mexican, Japanese, and Anglo-American residents had moved into Locke, and the total resident population was about 1,500. It was a place "along the river where laborers could come for Chinese food or a room between jobs or a woman or a night of gambling".[6]

If we examine the map of Locke in 1927, at the height of its boom, there is a clear economic and social center along Main Street. The number and locations of the gambling houses had changed since 1915, but in 1927, there was an agglomeration of activities of which gambling was a key part. Restaurants, social clubs, and theaters surrounded the main gambling house of Dai Loy. Farther away toward the ends of Main Street were grocery stores, drugstores, and lodging. Residents who mainly lived behind this commercial strip stressed the separation between Main Street and Key Street.

> At that time, Locke was a good place to raise children… Main Street never bothered us. Those people never go in the backstreet at all. It seems strange, we got bars here, but no drunks. You don't see them. If they do get drunk in the bars there on Main Street, we're all in bed already in the backhouse, we don't see them…. Even the people who come in on weekends, they don't even come near our Second Street.[7]

This sense of separation between residents and the transient population of workers and fun seekers was repeated in several accounts. There was an understanding that gambling and domestic life were distinct moral geographies. Yet, the two were also porous. Residents recalled how as children they would cleverly exploit the fast flow of money around these establishments by seeking handouts from lottery winners.

> There was a lottery every hour on the hour. When someone won an either-spot, the joint would set off a string of firecrackers…. Lottery winners could win nine hundred, a thousand dollars. Two hundred dollars maybe. Some of us kids would dash toward the place where the winner happened to be, waiting for a handout, knowing the winners liked to share their luck. Every store had its lottery tickets, you didn't have to go to the gambling halls to buy the lottery tickets.[8]

One of the gambling houses, Dai Loy, is now a museum. The architecture bears traces of the social practice of gambling and its transformation over time. Along a street dominated by two-story buildings, Dai Loy is a single-story building distinguished by its large, double doors and name sign. Yet, this double door cannot be opened—it is barred from the inside. At one corner is a bench in front of a smaller door leading into a vestibule and then into the gambling hall itself. From the inside, it is apparent that all the windows and side doors are similarly barred. Even the skylights have been covered and reinforced with wire mesh and steel bars.

That a large, inviting façade with double doors and a name that literally means "welcome" would actually be a fortress might seem paradoxical. Dai Loy transformed in response to security problems

posed by robbers and police in the 1920s.[9] When the police came to raid the gambling house, a sentry at the door would ring a bell inside the building. Thereafter, all the doors and windows would be bolted, while patrons continued gambling as silently as possible. Since police raids were often of a token nature involving a handful of arrests and the breaking of furniture but never permanent closure (until 1951), the architectural fortifications were developed over time to thwart police action on the one hand and to remain in place on the other. Several of the doors bear sledgehammer marks.

In the 1920s, gambling houses at Locke were a rigidly gendered space—women were never allowed to gamble there. In fact, internal screens were often set up to block the view of wives attempting to see whether their husbands were inside. Even after the Depression, only a few women were tolerated in Dai Loy. But for the majority of the male visitors and residents, Dai Loy was a welcoming place to socialize, relax, and find jobs. Today, at the front of the interior hall, one finds several tables of fantan and *pai gow*. A booth for the buying and drawing of lotteries is located in the center, and at the back are benches and tables where customers could relax, socialize, read Chinese newspapers and magazines, and play musical instruments provided by the house.[10] A map of China hangs on the wall. A stove shows where hot tea was prepared and served. One resident recalled some of the social functions of Dai Loy.

> Nobody has any postbox in town. Back of the gambling house there is a post slot where you can slip the papers in. You would come in town after a week on the ranch and look, you got a letter, you take it, it's yours…. Or a bunch of you might be horsing around playing pinochle back there, and somebody from Dennis Leary's ranch or Joe Blow's come up needing six guys to clean up and get ready for fruit picking…you go in there and see three of us sitting in there and you say, "Hey, you guys working?"… That's how they find you.[11]

Late Nineteenth-Century Macau

By the end of the nineteenth century, there were tanguans, or gambling houses that specialized in the game of fantan, all over the southern provinces of China, with Guangdong

Dai Loy interior.

Source: Kah-
Wee Lee, 2012

as its center of dissemination.[12] Prohibition was patchy, and local governments drew much revenue from the legalization of tanguans: between 1925 and 1931, fantan taxes yielded about 10 million yuan a year for Guangdong province, with total fiscal revenue for the year 1928 of 59 million yuan.[13] Historian Xavier Paulès estimates that by 1911 in Canton there were about 300 tanguans, though most were tiny, low-grade establishments and only about forty were proper, "deluxe" gambling houses. Due to the increasing criminalization of gambling in South China toward the 1890s, many tanguans were set up in Macau, where the Portuguese administration had legalized gambling. Out of all the monopolies, fantan was one of the most profitable for the Portuguese government

and Chinese operators. Between 1850 and 1879, taxation from fantan licenses grew from 9 percent of total government revenue to 34 percent, before stabilizing at around 20 percent at the turn of the century. Though the bidding process underwent several changes, primarily to maximize government revenue, licenses generally stipulated the amount of tax to be paid, the total number of tanguans or tables that could be in operation, and their locations.[14]

Two photographs show the exterior of a tanguan as seen from the street. They are prominently identified by large signs, lanterns, and ornate entrances but do not seem to be bigger or smaller than the surrounding buildings. These signs do not necessarily announce the building as a tanguan, but those that do would declare the grade of the establishment, based on a ranking system of silver and golden "plaques." Other signs advertise the buildings as an inn, tea house and restaurant, or by the company that runs the business. Lush balconies and awnings on the second stories establish these buildings as places of entertainment and luxury. As these images suggest, the tanguan was often found amid a cast of supporting commercial and social activities. Brothels, opium dens, pawnshops, hotels, and restaurants were the ancillary facilities that completed the gambling experience and industry.

Inside these gambling houses, one would find a gambling cross-section that cut across socioeconomic classes and colonial divides.

> The Chinese gambled alongside Westerners, Portuguese, British, and other Europeans, in the fantan halls or in the quiet of hotel rooms. Before the turn of the century, Camilo Pessanha was complaining of the small groups of British who prevented him from sleeping as they returned from their hotel rooms in the early hours of the morning after a fantan session.[15]

Though there were different grades of tanguan, the fact that the stakes of fantan were low meant that almost anyone could participate in the excitement of the game.[16] And unlike Locke, men and women visited the tanguans of Macau, and children could be found with their parents too. The atmosphere was rowdy and gamblers stood rather than sat around the table. Gamblers gambled against the house, thus creating "pleasurable feelings of empathy among the assembled gamblers."[17] This open antagonism between the house and the gambler is also captured in the opening image of this essay—the central banner on the wall declares the intention of the house to decimate all three sides (of the fantan table), while the left and right banners refer metaphorically to wealth entering the house.

Yet, social hierarchies did not completely dissolve around the gambling table. In a tanguan, there was only one big gaming table on the ground floor. However, there were two or three stories of balconies above the table. A visitor marvels at this strange sight in the 1920s.

> Fantan is the only game I know that is normally three stories high. There is a long table on the ground floor and above this, in the ceiling, is a hole of roughly the same dimensions. Above that, in the next ceiling, is another slightly smaller, hole. There are railings round the holes, and players are seated at them, their bets being lowered and their winnings raised in baskets, on strings, that are the size of deep fingerbowls.[18]

From these elevated positions, gamblers could observe the action and participate by placing their bets in little bowls or reed baskets that were lowered with ropes to the croupiers. Thus, there was a vertical social segregation where the poorer people gambled around the table and the richer gambled from above—this divide also kept the Europeans apart from the Chinese. Opium rooms adjoined the balconies on the upper floors, and snacks and drinks were readily available. This vertical segregation was also observed in other places of social interaction, such as the tea houses.[19]

This architectural model of gambling was also an economic ingenuity. It maximized the real estate of the gambling table, because the stacking of space allowed one table to service many more gamblers than was otherwise possible. It economized on manpower—since more tables would require more croupiers, accountants, and assistants, it was in the interest of the operator to keep the number of tables down while maximizing the number of gamblers. Possibly, more tables could also translate to more opportunities for cheating, as it would become increasingly difficult to supervise the exchange of money. Finally, since the Portuguese regulated the industry by controlling the number of tables, the table was the most precious real estate. It is not surprising therefore that the internal spatial organization of the tanguan was generated around this single piece of furniture.

Back to the Present

At the turn of the century, gambling in Chinese communities had to adapt to very different conditions. Criminalization and legalization not only changed how people gambled, they transformed the social and economic roles of gambling within a community. At Locke,

Tanguans in Macau, late
nineteenth century.

Source: Kah-Wee Lee

Tanguans in Macau, late
nineteenth century.

Source: Kah-Wee Lee

gambling was simultaneously a form of livelihood, social support, and leisure entertainment that had to be conducted in the permissive shadow of the law. Conflict between gamblers and residents of Locke was not unheard of, but recollections tended to downplay them and emphasized the role of Dai Loy as a stabilizing institution of the community.

In Macau, gambling houses materialized, adding to the leisure opportunities of clients, the colonial taxation regime, and the profitability of games. They were at the center of a much larger urban economy that tapped into and facilitated the hypercirculation of capital. As commercial establishments and the dominant industry of the colony, the tanguan contrasts with Dai Loy in its formalized spatial organization, where the commercial worth of clients was expressed in the vertical segregation of space and the grade of the tanguan itself.

These historical glimpses are worth considering today, as we try to understand how large-scale casino development is changing the social and physical fabric of cities such as Macau. Though Macau's preliberalization casino industry was a monopoly in name, in practice it was closer to a system of shared power sustained by ambiguous legalities and customary affiliations. This contrasts with the current oligopolistic system, where the flow of capital is largely monopolized by corporations and the government (though vested interests from the previous regime continue to operate in its interstices). This transformation is spatially registered in the dramatic increase in the size of developments, as well as their rejection of the urban context.

Where gambling houses a century ago were institutions embedded in the everyday lives of residents, supporting a host of small businesses just outside their doors, today's "integrated resorts," as their namesake suggests, are self-sufficient and insulated worlds that strive to keep the flow of capital within a buffer of legal injunctions and spectacular architecture. Money lost and won at the gambling tables is recycled through loyalty programs, "tandem activities" (an industry term for all the nongaming functions of an integrated resort that support the casino) and sophisticated financial services. In the name of "responsible gambling," social welfare, and good governance, this transformation is often cast in a narrative of progress.

We should not romanticize Dai Loy and the tanguans but use them to reflect critically on this simplified and self-serving narrative. One direction of this critical reflection, as I have shown, is in unpacking the relationship between institutionalized gambling and the urban context at multiple scales. Another is to problematize essentialist claims about the "Chinese gambler." Historical evidence points to how the moral and legal status of gambling is anything but static, and so too is the gambler as a subject. The important question is not whether such claims are true but whose interests are served when they are made.

This question loomed over the collective presentations of the 2016 G2E Asia conference. Though the casino economy had slumped amid the anticorruption drive by the Chinese government, industry experts reminded each other that Asia as a market is still underserved compared to the U.S. and that they should remain ready for the "Chinese millennials" just across the Macau border. More sophisticated and mobile than before, Chinese millennials would no longer be content with simulated destinations in Macau for they preferred to seek authentic experiences farther afield in Europe or the Americas. Yet, while acknowledging these changing habits, industry players held onto the essentialist refrain that "Asian people like to gamble." The corporate gaze may have shed the moralizing sting of the Orientalist gaze, but it nevertheless justifies itself by pretending to do no more than cater to the natural demand of a racialized demographic.

Crowded out by the industry, the "Chinese gambler," like the image that opened this essay, is once again frozen in a zone between the pathological, the mystical, and the eternal. The corporate gaze will look at this image and ask how to exploit the antagonistic relationship between the gambler and the house—which it believes characterizes the Chinese psyche—so as to make the games more exciting and profitable. It will never contemplate the possibility that this antagonism also functioned like a kind of "responsible gambling" program where the house did not mask its raw economic interest but displayed it as an open warning and challenge to all. This possibility has been foreclosed in the narrative of progress that serves the industry's interest.

Drawing from the London Illustrated News, 1909 shows Europeans gambling in a tanguan in Macau.

Source: Kah-Wee Lee

Notes

1. Thomas Braddell, "Gambling and Opium Smoking," *Journal of the Indian Archipelago*, New Series 1(1856):66–83.

2. "Taboos in Gambling in Macau Casinos," CLSA Asia-Pacific Markets, 27 July 2010:7.

3. See for example, Jasmine Loo, Namrata Raylu, and Tian Po S. Oei, "Gambling among the Chinese: A Comprehensive Review," *Clinical Psychology Review*, 28(7):1152–1166; and Fanny Vong, "The Psychology of Risk-Taking in Gambling among Chinese Visitors to Macau," *International Gambling Studies* 7(1) 2007:29–42.

4. Anti-Chinese sentiments grew in the 1870s in San Francisco, as racist politics and economic instability made Chinese coolies a perfect target for attack. Legislated prohibitions on buying and owning land were one of the many exclusionary policies enacted between the 1870s and 1940s in many states.

5. In fact, both the county sheriff and district attorney were gambling customers themselves. See Kathleen Graham, *Discovering Locke* (Walnut Grove, CA: Sacramento River Delta Historical Society, 1982), 4.

6. Calvin Trillin, "The Last Chinatown," *New Yorker*, 20 February 1978, 111; Gerardo C. Gambirazzio, *The Parallax View: Race, Land, and the Politics of Place-Making in Locke, California*, (Ph.D. Diss., University of California, Davis, 2009), 127.

7. Jeff Gillenkirk and James Motlow, *Bitter Melon: Inside America's Last Rural Chinese Town* (Berkeley, CA: Heyday Books, 2015), 76.

8. Ibid., 97

9. Jean Harvie, *An Account of Locke: Dai Loy Gambling Hall* (Walnut Grove, CA: Sacramento River Delta Historical Society, 1980).

10. Jean Bossi, "Lee Bing: Founder of California's Historical Town of Locke," *The Pacific Historian: A Quarterly of Western History and Ideas* 20(4) 1976:361.

11. Gillenkirk and Motlow, *Bitter Melon*, 35.

12. I am grateful to Xavier Paulès, who offered comments on a longer version of this paper. I have tried to build on his insights. All errors and misrepresentations are my own.

13. 胡根, 2009, 澳门近代博彩业史 (广东: 广东人民出版社), 122–198. [Hu Gen, 2009, Ao Men Jing Dai Bo Cai Ye Shi (Guangdong: Guangdong Renmin Chuban She), 122-198.]

14. 张廷茂, 2011, 晚清澳门番摊赌博专营研究 (广州:暨南大学出版社) [Zhang Ting Mao, 2011, Wan Qing Ao Men Fan Tan Du Bo Zhuan Ying Yan Jiu (Guangdong: Jinan Daxue Chuban She)]; Jorge Godinho, "A History of Games of Chance in Macau," Part 2: "The Foundation of the Macau Gaming Industry," *Gaming Law Review and Economics* 17(2) 2013:107–116.

15. Luís Andrade de Sá, "Ten Million Gold Coins," in *Macau Special* (Macau: Livros do Oriente, 1993), 172.

16. Xavier Paulès, "Gambling in China Reconsidered: Fantan in South China during the Early Twentieth Century," *International Journal of Asian Studies* 7(2) 2010:179–200.

17. Ibid., 193.

18. Christopher Rand, *Hongkong: The Island Between* (New York: Knopf, 1952), 97.

19. Qin Shao, "Tempest over Teapots: The Vilification of Teahouse Culture in Republican China," *Journal of Asian Studies* 57(4) 1998:1009–1041.

CHAPTER 6
MAY THE QI BE WITH YOU! FENG SHUI IN MACAU'S CASINOS

DESMOND LAM

Many Chinese people believe in feng shui, which posits that the earth, sky, and sea are full of qi, or force (positive or negative) that can be manipulated to one's advantage. Feng shui ("wind and water") is an ancient belief wherein one modifies the physical environment to influence events and to harmonize with one's surroundings. It often emphasizes the orientation or relationship of buildings and items within a building in relation to the five elements of metal, wood, water, fire, and earth. These five elements are used to manipulate the relationships between human beings, earth, and heaven.

Feng shui is closely associated with Taoism. Traditional Taoism centered on the human being and the natural environment, focusing on Tao or the Way. Later, Taoist priests moved increasingly towards using "magic" to enhance one's life through rituals and superstitions. Taoist religion includes not only the worship of gods but also the pursuit of longevity and immortality through special techniques. Taoist masters were early scientists and acted as mediums to the other world. As such, they appeal to the general public, making some of them almost semidivine. In general, Taoism predicates the relation of yin and yang, central but opposing forces in the universe that in turn give birth to the five basic elements mentioned above. Metal and water belong to yin, while fire and wood belong to yang. Earth is a neutral element. These concepts form the foundation for traditional Chinese medicine, the Chinese martial art of Tai Chi, and the art of feng shui.

For many years, Chinese people have designed their great architectural structures (e.g., imperial palaces) with a view toward the five elements. The subsequent feng shui is said to provide a significant influence on a person's life. For example, the feng shui of a person's tomb can have a deep effect on the lives (i.e., fortune and health) of descendants. While some Chinese are devoted to feng shui as a rational science, others see it as pure superstition. Still, most Chinese people accept it as part of the Chinese culture. The concept of feng shui reveals one key difference between Chinese and Western cultures: Chinese believe that humans are insignificant souls in this complex universe and should exist in harmony with it. They use feng shui to avoid bad fortune by keeping away negative qi and to increase the amount of fortune they get by bringing in positive qi.

Feng shui has had a tremendous effect on Chinese culture, which continues with modern Chinese people. Many Chinese in Singapore, Hong Kong, Macau, and China itself are still very much interested in this type of "science." Some pay thousands to feng shui masters to visit their home or office for advice on improving their feng shui. For example, before moving into a new apartment, a couple may seek advice from a feng shui master to calculate the best day and time for the move in, based on their birth dates. They may then sprinkle some rice grains onto the floor days beforehand in a ritual to banish all evil spirits. Others adhere to feng shui rules for what colors to wear on certain days and what

MGM Macau and Its
Golden Lion Statue.

Photo: Desmond Lam

Water and fire display
at Wynn Macau
with Hotel Lisboa in
the background.

Photo: Desmond Lam

gems to carry according to their personal Chinese zodiac signs. Many also believe in the potential for bad feng shui to affect personal lives negatively. In fact, research has found that residential and commercial prices in Hong Kong and Taiwan can be significantly affected by perceived bad feng shui.[1]

Several studies indicate that many Chinese people believe in good and bad luck.[2] Some even believe that there are winning streaks that are "unstoppable" because of one's immensely positive luck. In fact, in Macau's casinos, you will notice that on every gaming table people seem to be actively testing their luck. While some gamblers use their "abilities" to tap good luck, others piggyback on a winner's luck by betting at his or her side.[3] But although luck has an important role in Chinese gambling, belief in luck may be game-specific. According to research, it is more prevalent in the Chinese lottery and baccarat.[4] A simple Hokkien song from Singapore portrays the role of luck in lottery play among ordinary Chinese. Here is a portion of the English translated lyrics.

Some are born lucky, they can
lead a carefree life.
But don't compare our luck with
his as his numbers always win.
No matter how hard I work, I
can never be wealthy.
I've done no wrong, yet I always
miss by one digit.
· · ·
Some say the way to win is to be
faithful to your number.
I've stuck to my number for years, but only
have myself to blame for not buying it once.
What bad luck because that was
when it struck the first prize!

Casino floor designers in Macau appear to have done their research well to help enhance the perceived luckiness of their casinos. Often, it is the Chinese patrons themselves who add meaning to these "harmless" designs. There are many items, animals, and creatures that are considered more auspicious than others to the Chinese people. Auspicious creatures in Chinese mythology and belief include the dragon, phoenix, Tianlu and

Wynn Macau.

Photo: Desmond Lam

Bixie, Fu Dog (or keiloon), crane, lion, elephant, bat, frog, turtle, goldfish, and carp. The crane, for example, is a symbol of immortality and is often pictured with Taoist immortals. Pairs of lion statues can be found guarding the entrances of important buildings such as Buddhist temples. In Beijing's Forbidden City, the Hall of Supreme Harmony is decorated with dragons. The emperor is associated with the dragon, while the phoenix symbolizes the empress. Hence, the living quarters in the Forbidden City for the empress and concubines are decorated with phoenixes.

Among auspicious colors, red, gold/yellow, and green are the basic colors in the great Forbidden City. They are also often used to decorate Chinese temples. The emphasis on red in Chinese culture is said to originate from the Han period. In Buddhism, red symbolizes joy, gold/yellow symbolizes heavenly glory, and green symbolizes harmony. However, these colors are also significant to ordinary Chinese people in nonreligious ways and are often the preferred colors of choice in Macau's casino design. For example, the façades of the

Sands Macao and MGM Macau use gold color extensively. In addition, one need only take a short tour of the Wynn Macau to notice the excessive amount of red in its popular casino.

Indeed, Chinese people commonly equate red with happiness and celebration. It also represents auspiciousness or luckiness, vitality, love, reunion, and prosperity in modern Chinese culture. In feng shui, red is regarded as the most yang color. Its energy is expansive, which gives out positive qi. It is an important source of energy to ordinary Chinese people and gamblers. Among the five elements, red and green correspond to fire and wood, respectively. Earth is represented by yellow, which corresponds to fertility. Water is represented by black, and metal by white.

The influence of feng shui on casino architecture is most obvious in the large fountain at the front of the Sands Macao. To the ordinary Chinese, water symbolizes wealth. In this case, the fountain provides a perceived positive orientation of qi force that some patrons may feel is to their advantage. But more often than not, Chinese

Hotel Lisboa in Macau.

Photo: Desmond Lam

gamblers interpret such design as benefiting the casino. Similarly, hardly anyone can miss the splendid display of lights and fire at the musical fountain at the front entrance of the Wynn Macau, another perceived positive qi force for the casino, but perhaps secondarily for its patrons.

A feng shui master is said to have helped design every detail of the Sands Macao (as it is spelled) to ensure that all classical elements were in harmony. This includes the round beehive-shaped casino floor and the fifty-ton central chandelier. They are supposed to bring good luck to the Las Vegas-style casino, but according to the press and many industry observers, the chandelier looks like a giant beehive to retain and store the casino's "honey." A renowned feng shui master was specially invited from Taiwan to evaluate the feng shui in the Venetian Macao. The master reportedly identified numerous feng shui traps in the Venetian's shopping mall and suggested specific paths to enter its casino. The Wynn Macau's curvy roof had some people commenting that it looked like a hand opening to grab something or a knife ready to cut the "throat" of its patrons.

Interestingly, some feng shui masters believe the Wynn Macau designed its building to counteract the feng shui of the old Hotel Lisboa,

which stands opposite. Hotel Lisboa has been a successful casino for many decades. According to some, it looks like a birdcage, and the intention is to trap the "birds". Gamblers who go into the casino will get "trapped," and the casino "wins." Its bat-like main entrance is also supposed to bring wealth to the casino. Side entrances are built purposefully to allow some gamblers to "escape," since the casino would like them to come back in the future. It's not good to take everything from the Chinese gamblers all at once. Wynn's water-and-fire show, which occurs at regular intervals at its main entrance, is immediately across from Hotel Lisboa. The aim, according to feng shui experts, is to burn Lisboa's birdcage and, hence, destroy the feng shui of their competitor.

On the other side of the street, the new, majestic Grand Lisboa has a huge, pearl-like entrance hall. A feng shui expert claimed to have influenced the Grand Lisboa design, after taking into account the Wynn's qi elements, by suggesting a huge pearl building to represent treasure in front with the tall building representing authority behind. The building looks like a great metallic pineapple, an auspicious fruit (or item) to some Chinese dialect groups. In Hokkien, "pineapple" sounds like "prosperity is coming." Rumors claim that the Hotel Lisboa is

Chinese Gamblers in Macau.

Photo: Desmond Lam. Taken from a public area above the Venetian Macao-Resort-Hotel casino.

constantly under renovation because "renovation" in Cantonese sounds similar to "house collect" and that is why the management of Hotel Lisboa is delighted to keep renovating.

If nothing else, all these discussions and rumors cause one to realize how much Chinese actually think about and respond to feng shui, luck, and superstition, whether these affect them or not. More often than not, Chinese patrons and their feng shui masters adopt a rather negative stance toward casino architecture. Many suspect that casinos are built purposefully with many feng shui "traps." There is almost a collective focus on counteracting the effect of these designs with "special techniques" to gain luck so as to beat the house. Chinese gamblers gain confidence when they feel that they can successfully identify and neutralize these traps.

Thus, on the gaming floor, operators and patrons are often engaged in a smaller battle of luck, superstition, and feng shui. The number 4 was removed from all baccarat tables in Macau's casinos. Four, which means "dead" in Chinese, is taboo for many Chinese. Water that is used to channel qi has become a common feature in many of casinos (both within and outside) that welcome Chinese gamblers. Water helps to please the Chinese patrons and to soothe their gambling anxiety. Chinese gamblers are also on the lookout both for features that promote positive qi and for feng shui traps. Superstitious gamblers will carefully plan their gambling trips to maximize their luck. Using the Chinese zodiac, they select the right day and time to gamble. A book published in 2006 documented the feng shui for all of the casinos in Macau, listing the good and the bad of the feng shui at each, how to avoid bad feng shui, when to gamble, what color to wear, what gems to bring, and how to improve one's luck in order to win.[5] There are do-it-yourself formulae for winning, such as taking a special flower bath, nurturing a feng shui plant such as bamboo, and using color to improve luck. The book also offers special feng shui techniques to win in specific games like lottery, poker, horse racing, and baccarat. To gain more luck in a poker game, for example, one should go to a washroom, comb one's hair three times, and then wash one's hands or face. Individuals with certain Chinese zodiac signs are more suited to win at certain casinos. Ox, tiger, rabbit, snake, goat, and pig will do well at the Sands Macau; mouse, tiger, dragon, horse, dog, and pig will do well at Hotel Lisboa. In a 2011 sequel, readers get more information on how to tackle casino dealers, who are categorized by appearance.[6]

On a trip, some gamblers might look for specific locations within a casino that offers the best feng shui. Others would avoid the main casino entrance at all costs, since they think feng shui masters curse most main entrances. To combat these curses, some even bring along their own feng shui master to help figure a way to get in and beat the casino on the gaming table. The talented master will pick the right table for them, with the right dealer, and at the right time. Then, they will go in for the "kill." Others will simply bring their lucky talisman, three-legged frog, wealth coin, gem, or other objects they think will bring them better luck and fend off negative influences.

The strong emphasis on luck and feng shui in Macau's casinos has added a unique layer of mystique to this uniquely Chinese gaming entertainment city. Research has shown that the Chinese are avid and superstitious gamblers, with some treating their regular gambling trips as a form of investment.[7] To some, gambling is a job, and one must constantly try to gain the upper hand over the house using whatever legitimate methods one can employ. Whether it is for the good of the operators or patrons, publicized luck and feng shui elements in casinos and related facilities have added to the Macau buzz and contributed to its ballooning gaming revenue and rising tourist numbers year-on-year.

Notes

1. C. M. Tam, T. Y. N. Tso, and K. C. Lam, "A Study
of Feng Shui and Its Impacts on Land and
Property Developments: Case Study of a Village
Housing Development in Tai Po East Area,"
Urban Design International 3(4) 1998:185–193;
Lin, Chu-Chia, Chien-Liang Chen, and Ya-
Chien Twu. "An Estimation of the Impact of
Feng-Shui on Housing Prices in Taiwan—A
Quantile Regression Application," International
Real Estate Review 15(3) 2012:325–346.

2. D. Lam, "An Observation Study of Chinese
Baccarat Players," *UNLV Gaming Research
and Review Journal* 11(2) 2007:63–73; K.
Zhou, H. Tang, Y. Sun, G. H. Huang, L. L. Rao,
Z. Y. Liang, and S. Li, "Belief in Luck or in Skill:
Which Locks People into Gambling?" *Journal
of Gambling Studies* 28(3) 2012:379–391.

3. D. Lam, 2007.

4. Zhou et al., 2012.

5. Si Tu Fa Zheng, 大殺四方 (Hong
Kong: 博學天地, 2006).

6. Si Tu Fa Zheng, 龍年招財大全
(Hong Kong: 宇宙出版社, 2011).

7. D. Lam, D., and B. Ozorio, "An Investigation
into Chinese Betting Behavior," in *Psychology
of Gambling*, Marco J. Esposito, ed., (New York:
Nova Science Publishers, 2008); B. Ozorio and K.C.
Fong, "Chinese Casino Gambling Behaviors: Risk
Taking in Casinos vs. Investment," *UNLV Gaming
Research and Review Journal* 8(2) 2004:27–38.

CHAPTER 7

REASSESSING ECONOMIC SUCCESS: MORE THAN A DECADE AFTER CASINO LIBERATION IN MACAU

MIAO HE and RICARDO C. S. SIU

"What Las Vegas built in 40 years, Macau will build in 10."

— **Prentice Salter,**
   Financial Times, **6 September 2006**

Since the Macau Special Administrative Region (SAR) Government replaced the monopoly structure of its casino industry with an oligopoly on February 8, 2002, the industry has witnessed a period of dramatic expansion. Prior to 2002, there were only eleven casinos, all owned by the former gaming monopoly. By the end of 2014, the number of casinos had increased to thirty-five (a number of them are mega casino resorts rather than the traditional small-scale casino hotel), owned by six gaming concessionaires (i.e., gaming license holders).

Indeed, the rapid expansion of casino gaming has not only turned Macau into the world's largest casino jurisdiction (in terms of gross gaming revenue (GGR; $44.1 billion in 2014) but also contributed to the city's general prosperity. In addition, the progress of casino gaming has evidently boosted business opportunities for associated industries such as tourism and meetings, incentives, conventions, and exhibitions (MICE).

Nevertheless, the staggering performance of Macau's casinos is not without adverse effects on the local economy, and such frictions can be quite significant. In nominal terms, the share of casino gaming in the Macau economy has been expanding over time. In 2014, for example, the

amount of the GGR as a percentage of Macau's GDP was around 80 percent. Consequently, it was observed that the rapid expansion of casinos had exerted much pressure onto other business sectors, especially small and medium enterprises (SMEs) such as restaurants and retail shops. The different types of pressures include soaring labor and rental costs.

In addition, given that Macau's total geographic area is only about 30 square kilometers with residential population around 636,000 (2014), serious congestion and increasing pollution from over 31.5 million visitor arrivals put great stress on the local quality of life and threaten the idea of sustainable growth. Increasing competition from the East and Southeast Asian regions in casino gaming and tourism raises uncertainty regarding potential for long-term growth of Macau's casinos, although the near-term threat is mild.

Following the Portuguese handover of Macau at the end of 1999, it was in the public interest to ensure the development of this tiny economy as a "dynamic and prosperous centre" (BBC News, 12 Dec. 1999). Thus, the Macau SAR Government sought to redirect traditional and monotonic casino gambling toward a modernized and internationally competitive casino resort and leisure hub. By promulgating

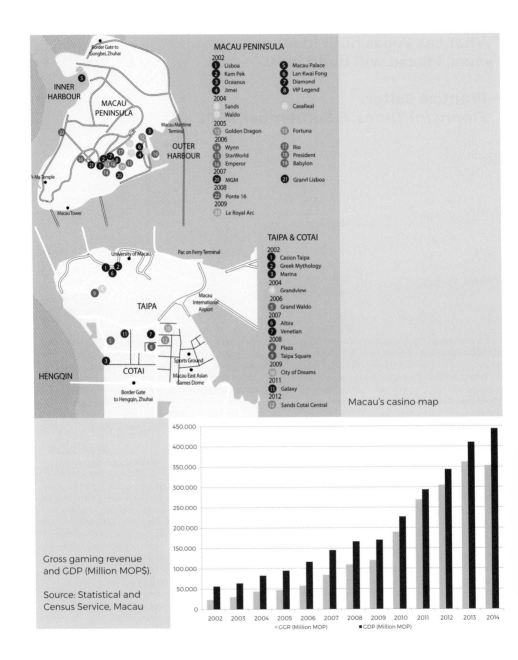

MACAU PENINSULA

2002
1 Lisboa
2 Kam Pek
3 Oceanus
4 Jimei

2004
9 Sands
10 Waldo

2005
12 Golden Dragon

2006
14 Wynn
15 StarWorld
16 Emperor

2007
20 MGM

2008
22 Ponte 16

2009
23 Le Royal Arc

5 Macau Palace
6 Lan Kwai Fong
7 Diamond
8 VIP Legend

11 CasaReal

13 Fortuna

17 Rio
18 President
19 Babylon

21 Grand Lisboa

TAIPA & COTAI

2002
1 Casion Taipa
2 Greek Mythology
3 Marina

2004
4 Grandview

2006
5 Grand Waldo

2007
6 Altira
7 Venetian

2008
8 Plaza
9 Taipa Square

2009
10 City of Dreams

2011
11 Galaxy

2012
12 Sands Cotai Central

Macau's casino map

Gross gaming revenue
and GDP (Million MOP$).

Source: Statistical and
Census Service, Macau

■ GGR (Million MOP)   ■ GDP (Million MOP)

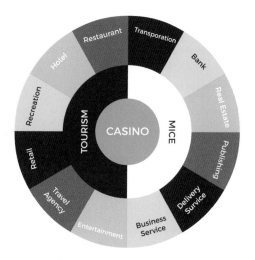

Casino related industry in Macau.

a new gaming law (Law 16, 2001), international casino resort operators were invited to bid on three new casino gaming concessions (Administrative Regulation no. 26/2001).

Given that under the Chinese government's "One Country, Two System" policy, Macau would be the only legal casino jurisdiction in China, the open bid attracted twenty-one world-class operators from the U.S., Australia, South Africa, etc. Ultimately, the Sociedade de Jogos de Macau (SJM), a wholly owned subsidiary of the former casino monopoly Sociedade de Turismo e Diversões de Macau (STDM), received the first concession. The second concession went to the Wynn Resort. Finally, the last concession was granted to Galaxy JV, a joint venture between Galaxy (a Hong Kong entertainment firm) and the Venetian of the Las Vegas Sands Corporation (and self-described pioneer in the "MICE-driven integrated hotel resort"). By approving these new casino licenses, it was commonly anticipated that the development of the MICE industry and a stronger, value-added tourism industry would also be kicked off.

But changes did not proceed according to the initial proposals of the three new license holders. By the end of 2002, the Macau SAR Government approved a split of the Galaxy and Venetian partners to construct separate operations.

KICKING OFF CHANGES SINCE 2002

FEBRUARY 8, 2002
3 new concessions were granted to SJM, Wynn, and Galaxy JV respectively

DECEMBER 2002
The split of Galaxy and Venetian was approved (the latter as a subconcession holder)

MAY 18, 2004
The first nonlocal casino (Sands Macao) opened

APRIL 20, 2005
MGM received a subconcession from SJM

SEPTEMBER 4, 2006
The first casino resort (Wynn Macao) opened

SEPTEMBER 8, 2006
Melco-PBL received a subconcession from Wynn (renamed Melco-Crown)

FEBRUARY 11, 2007
SJM's Grand Lisboa opened

AUGUST 28, 2007
The first mega casino resort (Venetian Macao) opened on Cotai Strip

DECEMBER 18, 2007
MGM Macao opened

AUGUST 28, 2008
Commencement of Venetian's Zaia show

JUNE 1, 2009
Melco-Crown's City of Dreams opened on Cotai Strip

KICKING OFF CHANGES SINCE 2002 (cont'd)

SEPTEMBER 16, 2010
Commencement of City of Dream's
House of Dancing Water show

MAY 15, 2011
Galaxy Macao opened on Cotai Strip

FEBRUARY 19, 2012
Close of Venetian's Zaia show

APRIL 11, 2012
Sands Cotai Central opened

MAY 27, 2015
Galaxy Phase 2 and Broadway Macao opened

OCTOBER 27, 2015
Melco-Crown's Studio City opened

Subsequently, the Venetian also was designated "subconcessionary" (i.e., a sublicense holder) in the development of Macau's new casino industry.

An Unexpected Push, 2003

Following Beijing's approval of Macau as a unique casino city in China, an Individual Visit Scheme (IVS) was introduced in the summer of 2003.This allowed mainland Chinese citizens from selected high-income cities to visit Hong Kong and Macau at their own discretion. Indeed, the IVS policy unexpectedly encouraged the dramatic expansion of Macau's casino industry from the demand side. The scheme spread, and by May 2004 the IVS included the entire Guangdong province. By the end of 2014, citizens from forty-nine cities were permitted to visit Macau. After the introduction of the IVS, mainland visitor arrivals significantly increased and soon surpassed visitors from Hong Kong. Beijing's support through the IVS also increased the resilience of Macau's economy to external shock. For example, the global financial tsunami in 2008–2009 appeared to have a much less impact on visitor arrival than the SARS (severe acute respiratory syndrome) outbreak in southern China in 2003.[1]

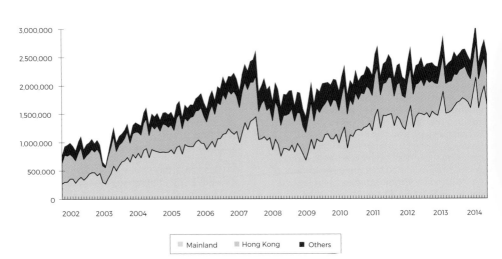

Number of visitor arrivals by citizenship.
Source: Statistical and Census Service, Macau

The Sands Effect, 2004–2005

On 18 May 2004, the first foreign casino—the Sands Macau—opened, a milestone that was not only ended the old casino monopoly but also introduced Las Vegas-style mass-market gaming. On opening day, around 30,000 people crowded into the Sands, impressed by the elegant environment, pleasant service, and exciting live shows. The new casino complex was immediately successful: it recouped the $240 million construction cost in just eleven months.

In contrast to other casino jurisdictions around the world, Macau's casinos are dominated by a particular form of third-party-operated gaming-room business, commonly categorized as "VIP baccarat" play under official statistics. A casino license holder can informally subcontract part of its business to a group of independent gaming agents (similar but not identical to the junket operators in international practices), who may utilize their own social networks to bring in patrons and run their businesses in the gaming (VIP) rooms inside the casinos. By contrast, the Las Vegas mass-market model targets walk-in customers, focusing more on visitor quantity than high rollers. But Beijing's support for mainland visitors under the IVS enabled the Sands to attract a high volume of traffic, proving the huge potential for mass-market development in Macau.

Gaming Expands, 2005–2006

In considering the Galaxy JV concession split, the Macau SAR Government further agreed that the other two concession holders could follow the same practice. Consequently, the SJM, the original post-monopoly concessionaire sold a subconcession through its joint venture to another major Las Vegas casino operator, the MGM. The Wynn sold another subconcession to Melco–PBL in 2006. The related changes from the three original gaming licenses to the ultimate approval of six operators (the "3+3" change) expanded the scale of Macau's casino industry to a scale unforeseen at the outset, both in terms of capital investment and the level of market competition.

The total fixed capital investment originally proposed by the three new concessionaires was around MOP$17.5 billion (Macau Pataca). Owing to the "3+3" arrangement, the scale of the capital investment by the six casino firms to the end of 2012 was at least six times the original proposal (accumulated volume of capital investment in related property, plant, and equipment by the end of 2012 amounted to MOP$111.3 billion). Indeed, capital investment is projected to double again when other new casino resort properties open between 2015 and 2018.

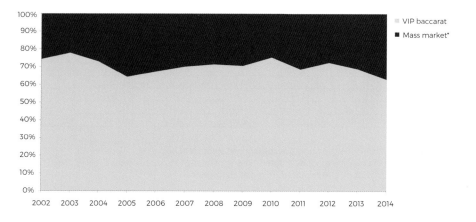

Proportion of VIP rooms vs. mass market in total table game revenue
Source: Gaming Inspection and Coordination Bureau, Macau
* Mass market refers to other table games aside from VIP baccarat

Tensions and Adjustments, 2007–2008

Given traditions of the gaming business and the nonproactive features of the regulatory system, the increasing number of competitors in the market led to significant tensions. Indeed, shortly after the opening of the Sands Macau, the commission offered to gaming agents and direct rebate to customers, which was different from the traditional practice of the local operators, led to complaints. For example, one operator declared that Sands "cutthroat" competition increased its own gaming agents' commission rate from around 0.8 percent of the chip rolling volume in 2002 to an average of 1.1 percent in 2006, which led to bankruptcy for some of the older junket operators.[2]

As competition for market share by increasing junket commissions was not well monitored or regulated, it went up to 1.35 percent (or even 1.40 percent) in the last quarter of 2007. This, indeed, exhausted the profit margins of casino concession holders for related gambling games, although the reported GGR from related gaming-room business also increased rapidly. In addition, irregular business activities evidently showed that the market might be at risk of spinning out of control.

To save the market from further chaos, Beijing took action to tighten the IVS in the first quarter of 2008, while the Macau SAR Government also intervened and placed a cap of 1.25 percent on the junket commission rate. As a result, the number of mainland visitors dropped significantly. Being further affected by the outbreak of the global financial crisis in the summer of 2008, the GGR from Macau's casinos showed a negative trend (on a year-to-year basis) from September 2008 to June 2009. Nevertheless, the casinos received a clear and credible message that market discipline must be well maintained to avoid similar repeated actions by these two governments.

Consolidation of Cotai's Nongaming Leisure and Entertainment since 2008

Restricted by the small landmass of the Macau peninsula, the possible scale of the development of nongaming leisure and entertainment facilities is somewhat limited. The opening of the Venetian Macao in Cotai in August 2007 marked an essential stage in consolidating large-scale, nongaming leisure and entertainment facilities and allowed Macau to be developed as a comprehensive, casino resort-destination. Finally,

Total investment (in property, plant, and equipment) of each casino firm (in Million MOP$, where 1USD = 8MOP)

Concession	SJM		Galaxy		Wynn		Total
Sub-con-cession		MGM		Venetian		Melco-Crown	
Contracted	4,734		8,800		4,000		17,534
2008	9,822	/	6,675	41,886	7,259	16,862	82,504
2009	10,444	/	7,391	39,412	8,784	22,293	88,323
2010	9,771	5,512	12,766	44,026	8,603	21,375	102,053
2011	9,041	5,114	17,993	49,998	7,924	21,243	111,312

Sources:
Contracted value: Gaming Inspection and Coordination Bureau, Macau
SJM: Property, plant and equipment, consolidated balance sheet, SJM Annual report, 2008, 2010,2011
MGM: Property and equipment, consolidated financial statement of financial position, MGM China annual report, 2011
Galaxy: Property, plant, and equipment, consolidated balance sheet, Galaxy annual report, 2009, 2011
Venetian: Net property and equipment, consolidated balance sheet, Sands China annual report, 2009, 2011
Wynn: Property and equipment and construction in progress, consolidated statement of inancial position, Wynn Macau annual report, 2009, 2011
Melco-Crown: Net property and equipment, consolidated balance sheet, Melco-Crown annual report, 2008, 2009, 2011

Macau had world-class facilities to support efforts to develop its MICE industry. (Cotai was a plot of almost empty land reclaimed between two small islands, Taipa and Coloane, in the mid-1990s.)

As a pioneer in this progress, the well-known Cirque du Soleil resident show, *Zaia*, from Las Vegas, was also introduced to the Venetian Macao in the summer of 2008, in a custom, 18,800-seat theatre. But despite the Venetian's international brand, *Zaia* failed to impress Chinese audiences. Only 30 percent of its seats filled in the beginning. Although the show was later redesigned to include some Chinese-style elements, like a lion dance and a flying dragon, attendance only increased to around 60 percent of capacity.

In contrast, a tailor-made show introduced in 2010 at Melco-Crown's City of Dreams, *The House of Dancing Water*, received rave reviews from Chinese visitors. Indeed, the new show incorporated culture elements that were particularly appealing to audiences from China and Asia. On the other hand, the Venetian terminated *Zaia* in 2012.

In addition to the eye-catching features and facilities constructed by the Venetian and Melco-Crown, another milestone in Cotai's development was unarguably the opening of the Galaxy Macau in May 2011. Hailed as The New Palace of Asia, this mega casino resort featured an artificial beach and wave pool, complemented by unique accommodation and retail facilities.

Considering the Cotai's success and its location adjacent to Hengqin Island, now approved for development, the other three casino resort operators (SJM, Wynn, MGM) also obtained approval from the Macau SAR Government to join in the fun in Cotai. It is anticipated that when their new facilities open between 2016 and 2018, Macau's development will have definitely entered another exciting era.

Regional Competition Moving Ahead

Of course, the fabulous profits reported by Macau's casinos in the short decade following liberalization have caught the attention of governments and existing operators in East and Southeast Asia. Many have been reconsidering the role of casino gaming in their own nations. For example, Singapore approved a casino bill in 2005. Subsequently, the impressive performance of its two casino resorts (the Integrated Resorts) since opening in 2010 has undoubtedly proved the existence of a huge, relatively untapped market in this part of the world.

Following the successes of Macau and Singapore, Taiwan also passed a casino law in 2011. Although a local referendum on Penghu Island had voted down a proposal for a casino resort there in 2009, an alternative in Matsu was approved in 2012. In the Philippines, PAGCOR, the government-owned Philippines Amusement and Gaming Corporation, approved establishment of an "entertainment city" on a piece of reclaimed land in Manila Bay. In this proposal, four casino resorts are to be developed, and one license holder will subcontract its casino operations to Melco-Crown of Macau. Active expansion plans are also underway in South Korea. In addition to the recent expansion of the country's largest mega casino resort (the Kangwon Land), the Caesars Entertainment Corporation from Las Vegas has won the license for a joint venture with Indonesia's Lippo Group to establish a $696 million casino resort in Incheon.

In Japan, despite a years-long legalization process, it is widely anticipated by market participants that owing to a number of internal economic issues, the government will eventually approve a casino gaming bill. Although a recent legalization bill timed for the 2020 Tokyo Olympics failed, Japan is inevitably on the road. According to a projection by investment bank CLSA, casino gaming was likely to be legalized before 2025. In terms of annual GGR, it would be a $40 billion market. Indeed, Japan passed its casino bill by end of 2016.

Thus, it is evident that even though the capacity of the Asian market for casino gaming is large, competition from various nations for gaming revenues is also increasing. Despite the fact that Macau has the advantage of being first, and is supported by policies of the Chinese and Macau SAR governments, continuous and proactive measures to maintain its competitive power are essential.

Frictions Accompanying Rapid Growth and Prospects

As discussed, a decade of casino liberation in Macau has unarguably led to great and direct

CASINO REVENUE COMPOSITION 2002-2011

Since the 2002 end of Macau's gambling monopoly, six companies vie for a share of the growing casino market, which still largely depends on income from gambling rather than other revenue.

*Other revenue is composed of hotel, interest, catering, remittance, etc.

Source: Macau Gaming Inspection and Coordination Bureau Report

In million MOP$, where 1USD = 8MOP

Infographic: Chen Jun

A	SOCIEDADE DE JOGOS DE MACAU
B	WYNN
C	GALAXY ENTERTAINMENT
D	MELCO-CROWN
E	MGM
F	SANDS

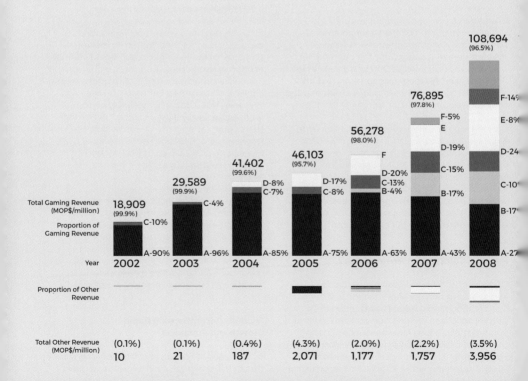

	2002	2003	2004	2005	2006	2007	2008
Total Gaming Revenue (MOP$/million)	18,909 (99.9%)	29,589 (99.9%)	41,402 (99.6%)	46,103 (95.7%)	56,278 (98.0%)	76,895 (97.8%)	108,694 (96.5%)
Proportion of Gaming Revenue	C-10% A-90%	C-4% A-96%	D-8% C-7% A-85%	D-17% C-8% A-75%	F D-20% C-13% B-4% A-63%	F-5% E D-19% C-15% B-17% A-43%	F-14% E-8% D-24% C-10% B-17% A-27%
Year	2002	2003	2004	2005	2006	2007	2008
Total Other Revenue (MOP$/million)	(0.1%) 10	(0.1%) 21	(0.4%) 187	(4.3%) 2,071	(2.0%) 1,177	(2.2%) 1,757	(3.5%) 3,956

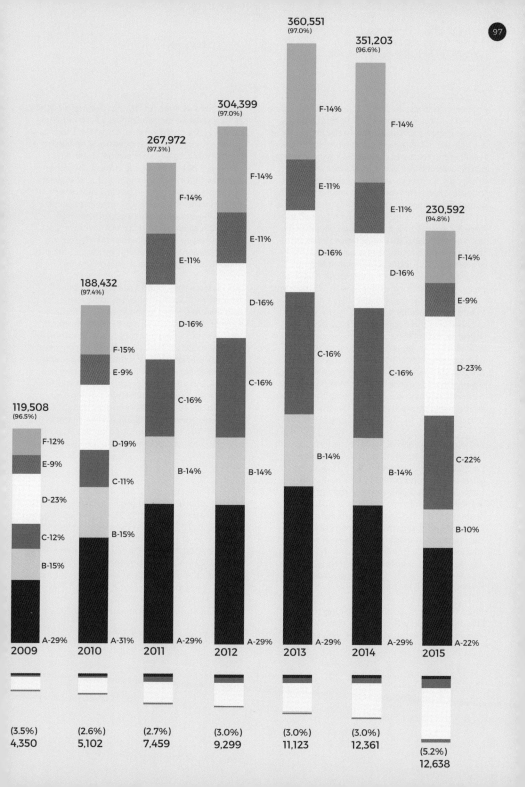

119,508
(96.5%)

F-12%
E-9%
D-23%
C-12%
B-15%
A-29%

2009

188,432
(97.4%)

F-15%
E-9%
D-19%
C-11%
B-15%
A-31%

2010

267,972
(97.3%)

F-14%
E-11%
D-16%
C-16%
B-14%
A-29%

2011

304,399
(97.0%)

F-14%
E-11%
D-16%
C-16%
B-14%
A-29%

2012

360,551
(97.0%)

F-14%
E-11%
D-16%
C-16%
B-14%
A-29%

2013

351,203
(96.6%)

F-14%
E-11%
D-16%
C-16%
B-14%
A-29%

2014

230,592
(94.8%)

F-14%
E-9%
D-23%
C-22%
B-10%
A-22%

2015

(3.5%)
4,350

(2.6%)
5,102

(2.7%)
7,459

(3.0%)
9,299

(3.0%)
11,123

(3.0%)
12,361

(5.2%)
12,638

economic success. Indicators such as the volume of fixed capital investment, GGR, local job opportunities, income added to the economy as a whole (i.e., GDP growth), as well as government revenue can testify to the success. Nevertheless, rapid success is not without adverse effects and implicit costs to certain economic groups. Indeed, it has been widely reported that due to competition from the new casino resorts in the factor markets, many local SMEs have suffered from increasing rental costs and shortages in both quantity and quality of labor. For example, the total employment in the gaming sector represented around 10.5 percent of Macau's employed population in 2004, while this proportion had doubled by 2014 to 21.5 percent.

In addition, partially propelled by the rapid expansion of the casino resort industry, domestic inflation has also increased to a relatively high level (5.5 percent in 2013, 6.05 percent in 2014), which has lowered the real standard of living for many families despite the rise in nominal income. Moreover, congestion and pollution following the dramatic increase in visitor arrivals have contributed to deterioration in the local quality of life.

Although the physical scale of the industry has significantly expanded, the progress of necessary complementary factors, such as infrastructure and quantity and quality of labor force, is lagging. Further, the industry's achievement in terms of external economies of scale may need to be further strengthened. To be a competitive gaming, tourism, and leisure destination, it is evident that the mere success of a *House of Dancing Water* or a New Palace of Asia may be insufficient. In other words, a series of signature, nongaming attractions still needs to be strategically planned.

To conclude, it is worth highlighting that the dramatic growth of casino gaming, and the admirable expansion of the nongaming

attractions as financed by the gaming profit since 2002, could be categorized as a kind of policy-backed growth. Given that it is subject to change in such policies, it is not necessarily sustainable. For example, there is occasional tightening of the IVS policy. And government control on the flow of funds from mainland to Macau on occasion has led to unexpected slowdowns. Following critical policy changes introduced by the Beijing and Macau governments in mid-2014 to rectify and control controversial and widespread irregularities on the part of gaming agents, progress of the casino industry (as well as the overall economy) slumped.

Yet, despite the uncertainties, progress in developing Macau into a "world tourism and leisure center" in the Pearl River Delta Economic Region (PRD) will not be reversed. Indeed, the casino industry may enter another era (mass tourism instead of the VIP segment, increased engagement with the nongaming hospitality segments). In this era, most of the existing infrastructure projects for promoting economic cooperation between the major cities in the PRD will be gradually completed from 2018 forward. Macau's related projects to link with the larger economic circle of the PRD are also proceeding on a similar timeframe.

Notes

1. In the SARS period, there were three consecutive months of decrease in visitor arrival (March–May 2003). The largest decrease was in April 2003, when the visitor arrival decreased 31.2 percent after the previous month. The 2008–2009 global financial recession, however, did not create any consecutive decreases, and the largest decrease was only 18.2 percent in September 2009. Note that the sharp decrease in January 2008 is due to the changed statistical criteria used by DSEC.

2. *Asia Times*, September 6, 2006.

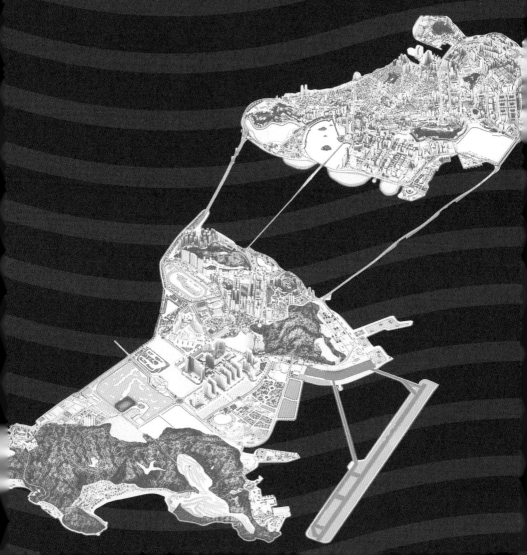

CATALOG
CASINOS IN MACAU

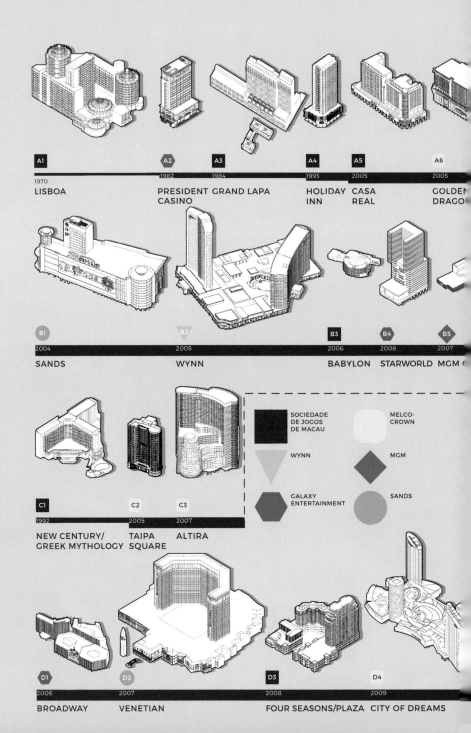

A1
1970
LISBOA

A2
1982
PRESIDENT
CASINO

A3
1984
GRAND LAPA

A4
1993
HOLIDAY
INN

A5
2005
CASA
REAL

A6
2005
GOLDEN
DRAGO

B1
2004
SANDS

B2
2005
WYNN

B3
2006
BABYLON

B4
2006
STARWORLD

B5
2007
MGM

C1
1992
NEW CENTURY/
GREEK MYTHOLOGY

C2
2005
TAIPA
SQUARE

C3
2007
ALTIRA

SOCIEDADE
DE JOGOS
DE MACAU

MELCO-
CROWN

WYNN

MGM

GALAXY
ENTERTAINMENT

SANDS

D1
2006
BROADWAY

D2
2007
VENETIAN

D3
2008
FOUR SEASONS/PLAZA

D4
2009
CITY OF DREAMS

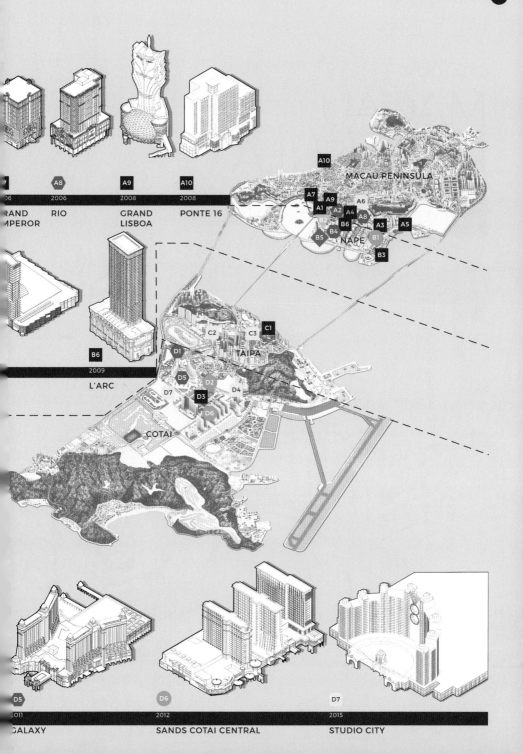

06
2006
GRAND
MPEROR

A8
2006
RIO

A9
2008
GRAND
LISBOA

A10
2008
PONTE 16

MACAU PENINSULA

A10

A7
A1

A9
A2
A4
A8
A6

B2
B6
A3
A5
B4
B1

B5
NAPE

B3

B6
2009
L'ARC

C2
C3
C1

D1
TAIPA

D5
D7
D2
D4
D3
D6

COTAI

D5
011
GALAXY

D6
2012
SANDS COTAI CENTRAL

D7
2015
STUDIO CITY

CATALOG A

MACAU PENINSULA

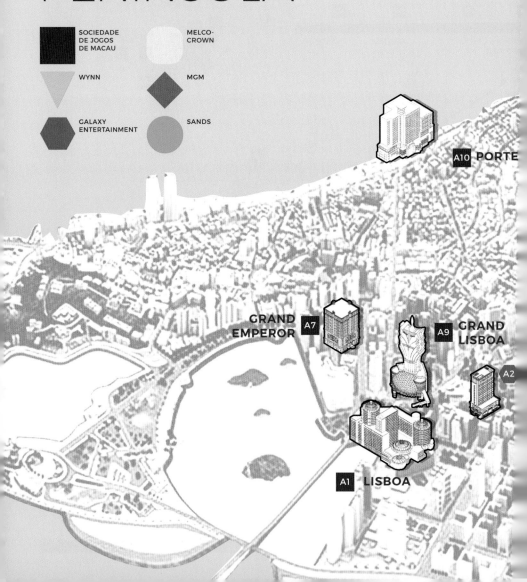

- SOCIEDADE DE JOGOS DE MACAU
- MELCO-CROWN
- WYNN
- MGM
- GALAXY ENTERTAINMENT
- SANDS

A10 PORTE

GRAND EMPEROR A7

A9 GRAND LISBOA

A2

A1 LISBOA

ENT

A4 **HOLIDAY INN**

A8 **RIO**

A6 **GOLDEN DRAGON**

A5 **CASA REAL**

A3 **GRAND LAPA**

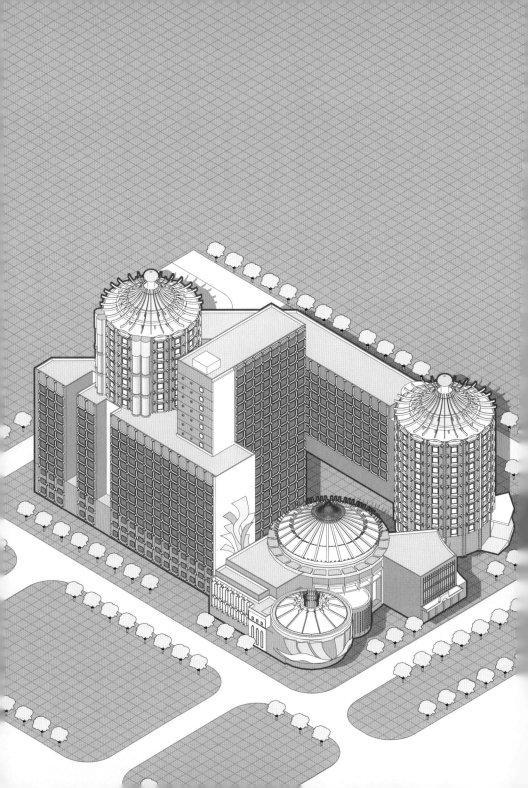

A1

CASINO LISBOA

YEAR OPENED:
1970

ROOMS:
927

OPERATOR:
SOCIEDADE DE
JOGOS DE MACAU

HEIGHT:
80 m

Hong Kong businessman Stanley Ho built the Casino Lisboa in 1970, then the city's largest hotel. The pastel-orange complex is covered in white, ornate moldings that appear to be a baroque, colonial-Portuguese interpretation of the screens of modern architect Edward Durell Stone. But a conical shape that reminds one of a pagoda tops the main, twelve-story cylindrical building. Some Chinese gamblers see the complex, because of its round shape and grille of moldings, as a vast birdcage designed to trap gambling "birds," but cylinder-shaped hotels were common in the 1960s, such as Chicago's Marina City, and so were stone screens.

Fueled by Macau's success as a tourist destination, the Lisboa grew four times its original size. Yet, the Lisboa remains a true Sino-Portuguese casino classic, with neon lotus petals marking the entrance, and a lobby featuring Ho's private art collection, including ancient Chinese jade artifacts.

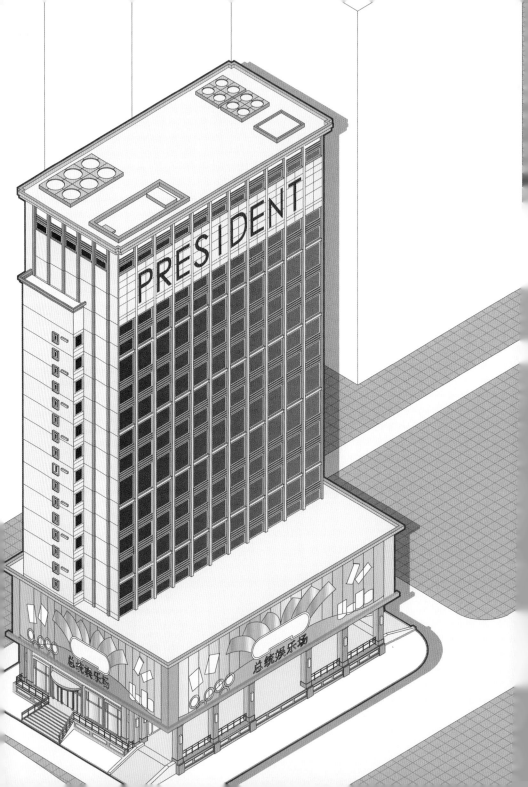

A2

PRESIDENT

YEAR OPENED:
1982

ROOMS:
212

OPERATOR:
GALAXY ENTERTAINMENT
GROUP

HEIGHT:
80 m

The President opened in 1982 as a hotel only and installed a casino in 2006 amid a celebration that featured the world's longest fireworks display, banging for a total of seven hours. A bizarre neon sign with a sic bo board (a Chinese game of chance) and a baccarat board decorated the new casino base and clashed with the modernist style of the hotel tower on top and the adjacent office buildings.

Today, the neon sign has been replaced with a simpler LED display with only the casino's name, giving the building a seriousness and symmetry reminiscent of a modernist Chinese communist headquarters.

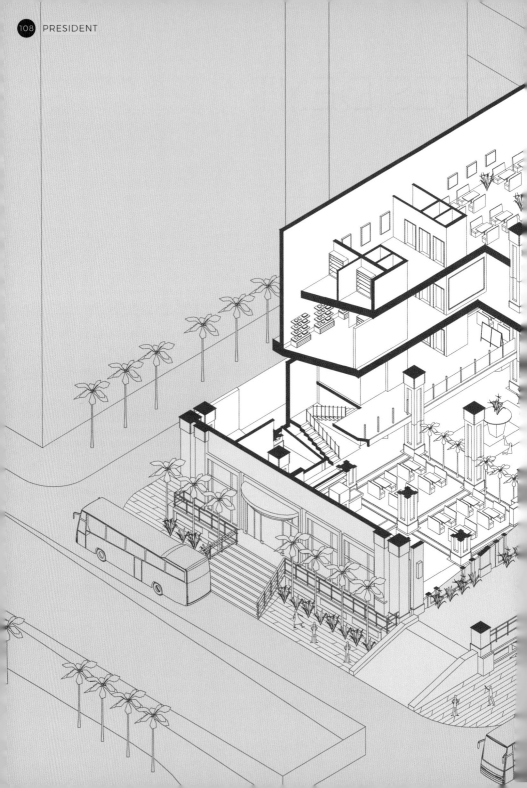

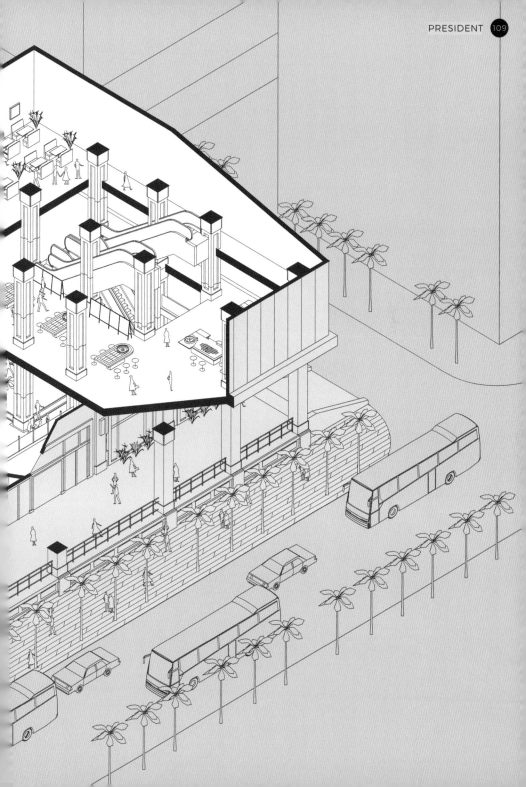

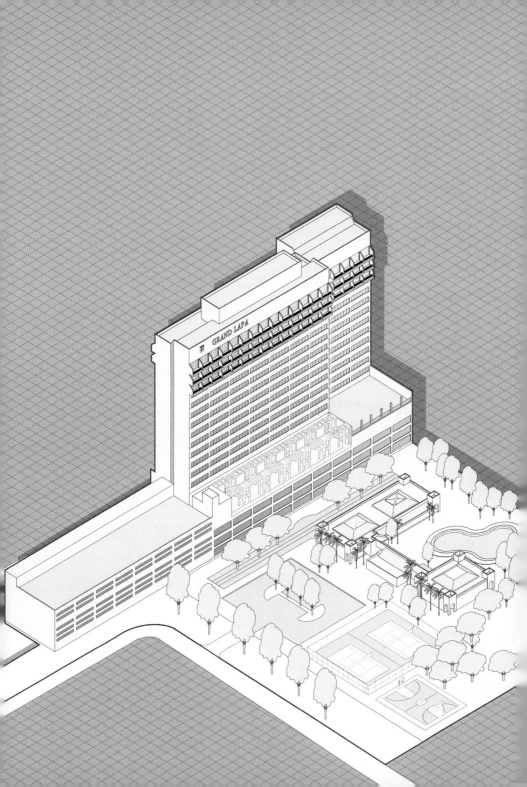

A3

GRAND LAPA

YEAR OPENED:
1984

ROOMS:
416

OPERATOR:
SOCIEDADE DE
JOGOS DE MACAU

HEIGHT:
60 m

In contrast to other Macau Peninsula casinos, the Grand Lapa's exterior lacks ornaments and has little external lighting. The tower has a simple, rectangular shape that widens at the top to accommodate suites with private balconies. It inherited its understated yet luxurious identity from being the former Mandarin Oriental. But the minimalism stops at the entrance; it has a lobby with polished woodcarvings, crystal chandeliers, and a sweeping staircase. The pool features pastel-orange spa buildings with arched doorways, inspired by sixteenth-century, colonial-Portuguese architecture.

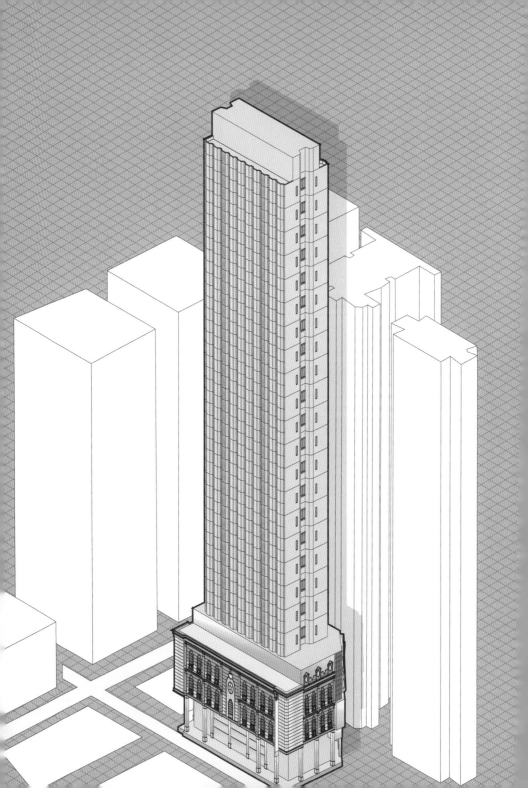

A4

HOLIDAY INN

YEAR OPENED:
1993

ROOMS:
323

OPERATOR:
SOCIEDADE DE JOGOS
DE MACAU

HEIGHT:
83 m

The Holiday Inn's architecture expresses the divided operations between the hotel — a mirror-clad, modernist tower — and the SJM-operated Diamond Casino, an ornate, colonial-Portuguese base, enhanced with Chinese signage. The architecture of the Rio and President also reflect this operational division, common to Macau's older casino hotels.

The corner-entrance features a three-story copy of Paris's Moulin Rouge pink windmill on top of an LED screen depicting a golden diamond. To beckon to passersby, the sign pulsates and changes color nonstop, bathing the adjacent residential buildings in all the hues of the rainbow.

A5

GOLDEN DRAGON

YEAR OPENED:
2005

ROOMS:
483

OPERATOR:
SOCIEDADE DE
JOGOS DE MACAU

HEIGHT:
59 m

The geometry of the Golden Dragon's two mirror-clad, hotel towers is articulated with lighter ribbons reminiscent of a 1980s Tokyo office building. The corners of the corporate-modernist-style building are wrapped in LED Chinese characters with meanings such as "heaven" to draw in customers, simultaneously pouring blinding light on neighboring apartment buildings.

The lobby features a golden ceiling and a floor mosaic with fish-like shapes — a *feng shui* symbol of prosperity.

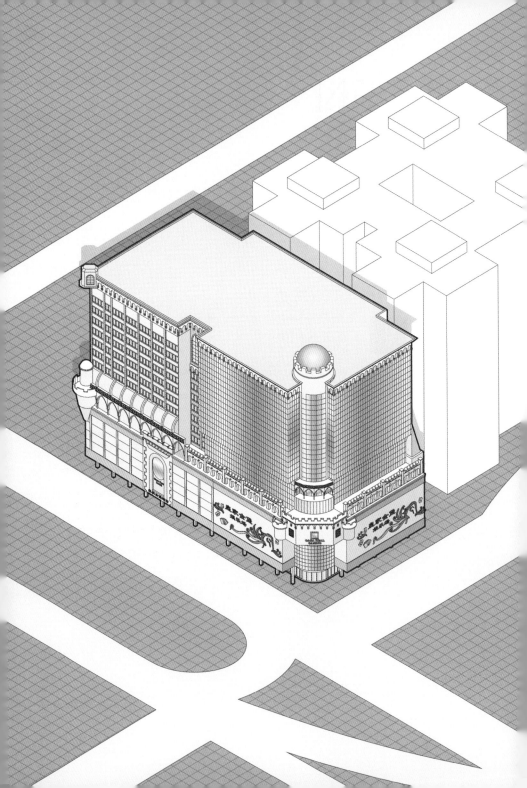

A6

CASA REAL

YEAR OPENED:
2005

ROOMS:
381

OPERATOR:
SOCIEDADE DE JOGOS
DE MACAU

HEIGHT:
52 m

Casa Real appears to be an odd hybrid between a corporate-modernist department store and a medieval Portuguese castle: the gold-clad box is decorated with late-Gothic arches, turrets, and crenelated walls. The rounded corner entrance is a throwback to the 1850s Paris Bon Marché.

Both the lobby and pool boast floors inlaid with *azulejos* — traditional, blue-tinted, ceramic Portuguese tiles. Yet these tranquil interiors contrast with the casino's three-story LED screen, which forced neighboring residents to install blackout curtains.

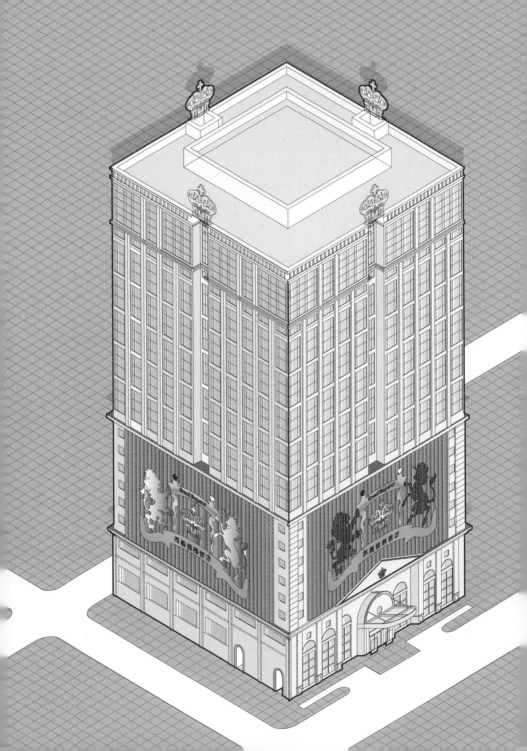

A7

GRAND EMPEROR

YEAR OPENED:
2006

ROOMS:
307

OWNER:
SOCIEDADE DE JOGOS
DE MACAU

HEIGHT:
80 m

The Grand Emperor brings eighteenth-century royal Britain to Macau. Men dressed up in Buckingham Palace-style uniforms perform a "changing of the guards" in front of an antique golden carriage. A pathway crossing over a display of seventy-eight bars of pure gold leads guests to a lobby featuring paintings of English royalty.

But the tower's symmetrical classicism evokes early skyscrapers, such as Louis Sullivan's Prudential Building (1896). A three-story LED screen wraps around the building, depicting two lions holding a crown. The casino alone occupies six entire floors.

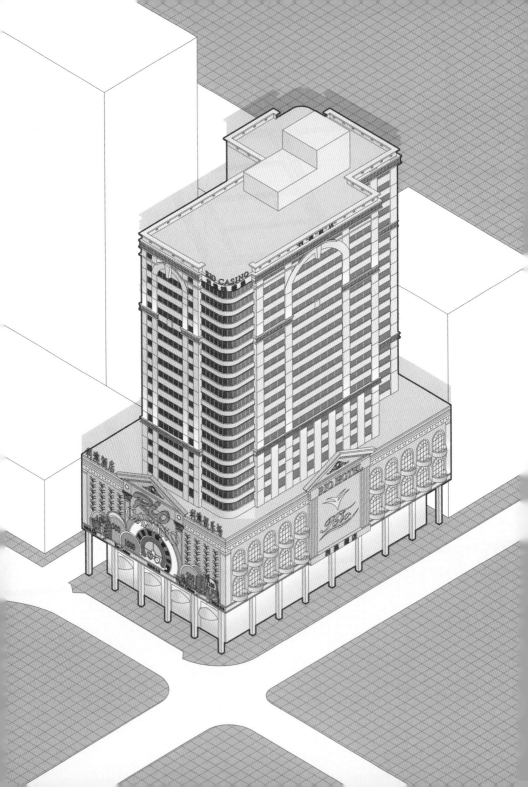

A8

RIO

YEAR OPENED:
2006

ROOMS:
450

OWNER:
GALAXY ENTERTAINMENT
GROUP

HEIGHT:
83 m

Over-scaled neoclassical arches, architraves and cornices decorate the Rio's twenty-four-story postmodern hotel tower. The casino-base evokes an oversized neoclassical palace, thanks to a Roman temple front, almost like architect Ricardo Bofill's massive housing estates, but enhanced with LED signage depicting casino chips and a roulette table. The hotel lobby has the obligatory marble floors and wood paneling. But the casino entrance provides a more extravagant passage, with a grand escalator pulling guests past fake arches underneath Italian frescoes and Renaissance-style carvings.

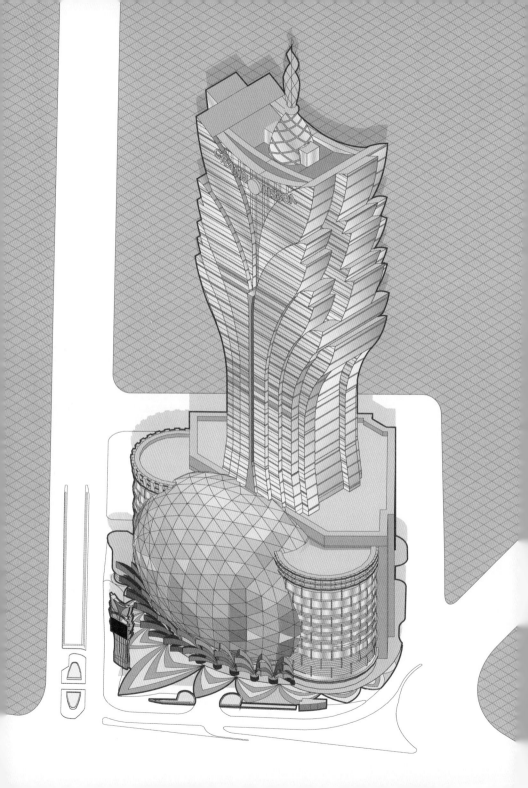

A9

GRAND LISBOA

YEAR OPENED:
2008

ROOMS:
430

OWNER:
SOCIEDADE DE
JOGOS DE MACAU

HEIGHT:
261 m

Hong Kong architect Dennis Lau wanted to design the Grand Lisboa not as another "veneered box" casino-hotel: a building squarish in shape with independently applied signage. Instead, he housed the casino in a massive orb covered in a mosaic of LEDs, as ornate as a Fabergé egg. On top of it, he built a hotel tower shaped after the feathered headdress of a Brazilian carnival dancer, although the sprouting plumes also evoke the petals of a lotus flower, Macau's emblem, as well as the Art-Deco frozen fountain motif. Despite these intentions, the two shapes together, both clad in gold, give the postmodern structure the look of a forty-seven-story pineapple.

The huge Grand Lisboa is considered the comeback casino of Stanley Ho, who used to hold the monopoly on gambling but saw his market share drop when foreign, rival casinos entered Macau. Circular ceiling domes in the lobby pay homage to the Lisboa, his 1970 casino. The lobby display features invaluable sculptures of jade, gold, and ivory, including the world's largest cushion-shaped diamond at 218 carats, and an intricately carved mammoth tusk depicting the story of the Monkey King, with hundreds of minuscule monkeys.

Photo: Alice Weng Sam Iu

**LOCAL MALE RESIDENT,
35 YEARS OLD**

"I personally dislike the Grand Lisboa as it seems far too intrusive to the old city center of Macau. The blinding LED lights cause a lot of light pollution to the surrounding neighborhood, particularly to the residential directly opposite. I have a friend who lives there, right next to the Bank of China, and she must have her curtains shut 24/7 together with added layers to her curtain fabric to block off the flashing lights.

However, we must admit that Grand Lisboa does bring a few benefits to us personally. Its free shuttle bus service for example is one of the main benefits that we as locals take advantage of. Those of us who live within close proximity are able to get to the ferry terminal directly at no cost whenever we want to make quick day trips to Hong Kong.

Hardly any locals gamble in Macau actually, so we locals usually only make use of the restaurants and bars since they provide quite a selection of fine and casual dining. The Grand Buffet is reasonably priced and provides a huge selection of food choices from all over the world, where I tend to bring my foreign friends to whenever they pay me a visit. The Noodles and Congee Corner is also rather special, as it serves good quality and a wide selection of Chinese noodles, as well as tea in traditional Chinese tea bowls. My foreign friends are often intrigued by the tossing and turning of the teapot skills of the tea pourer with the special brass teapot, plus the spectacular noodle-making skills of the chefs, as can be witnessed from the glazed kitchen where each bowl of noodles is made to order."

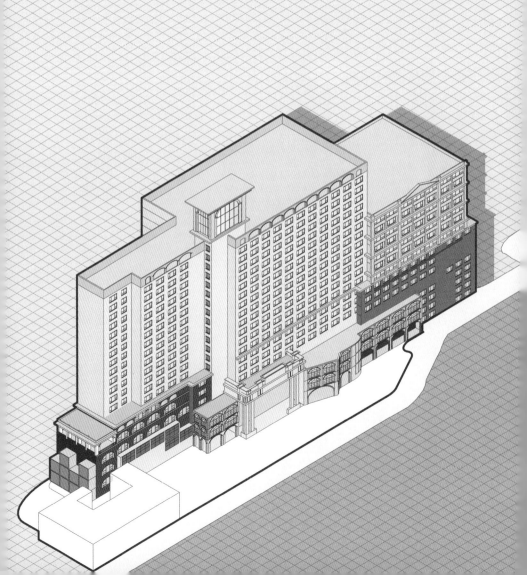

A10

PONTE 16

YEAR OPENED:
2008

ROOMS:
408

OWNER:
SOCIEDADE DE
JOGOS DE MACAU

HEIGHT:
59 m

Ponte 16 overlooks Macau's inner harbor, the only casino located on the northern part of the peninsula. Jon Jerde, the architect of the Las Vegas Bellagio, broke the mass of the sixteen-story tower into various pastel-colored "buildings" to make the colossus fit in better with its four-story surroundings. By over-scaling the cornice, he gave the colossus a horizontal feel. The asymmetrical composition with a tower is typical of Italian Renaissance, but the colors and details evoke sixteenth-century colonial-Portuguese architecture. The interior features undulating floor mosaics typical of Macau's historic plazas.

But the casino also has some 1980s glitz, thanks to a massive LED disco ball at the entrance, as well as a Michael Jackson gallery that boasts a rhinestone encrusted glove, used in the King of Pop's first moonwalk.

CATALOG B

NAPE
(NOVOS ATERROS DO PORTO EXTERIOR)

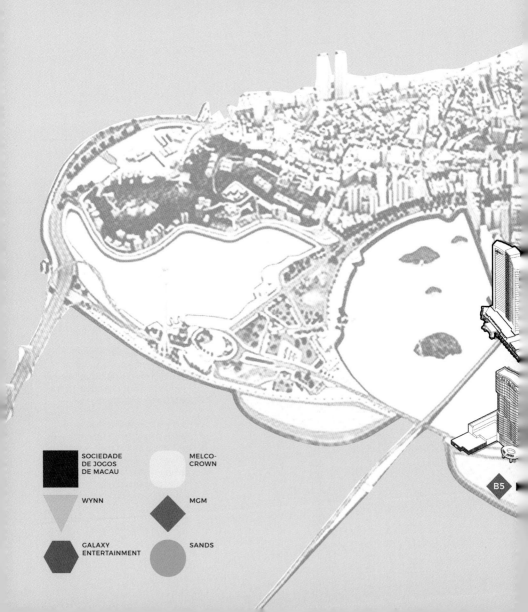

SOCIEDADE
DE JOGOS
DE MACAU

MELCO-
CROWN

WYNN

MGM

GALAXY
ENTERTAINMENT

SANDS

B5

MACAU PENINSULA

B2 WYNN/ENCORE

B6 L'ARC

B1 SANDS

B4 STARWORLD

B3 BABYLON

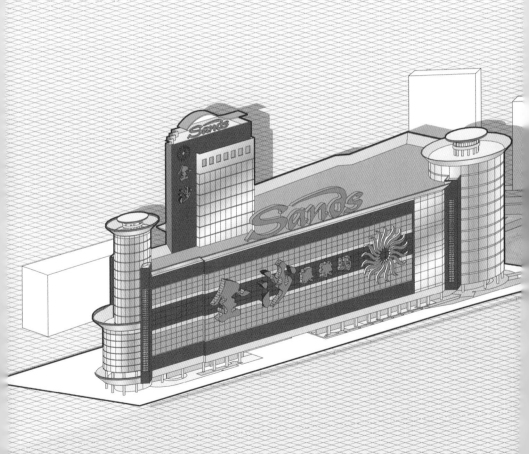

B1

SANDS

YEAR OPENED:
2004

ROOMS:
289

OPERATOR:
LAS VEGAS SANDS

HEIGHT:
79 m

American architect Paul Steelman designed the Sands, Macau's first foreign-owned casino, on land that the government had initially designated for a waterfront park. Departing from existing gambling dens, such as the Lisboa with its dark spaces and low ceilings, the Sands was the first "stadium-style" casino with a cavernous, daylit interior featuring a 50-ton chandelier hanging from a five-story-high ceiling. It also introduced a few Las Vegas casino characteristics: a higher level of service, an all-you-can-eat buffet, and easier automobile access, thanks to a four-lane *porte-cochère* and separate bus entrance.

Designed and built in a record period of only two years, the massive building has a plain geometric composition like a convention center or a big box store, built out of several separate geometric elements, including two gilded, cylindrical towers. Nevertheless, it was so successful that it paid for itself in only eight months, spurring more foreign gambling corporations to place their chips on Macau.

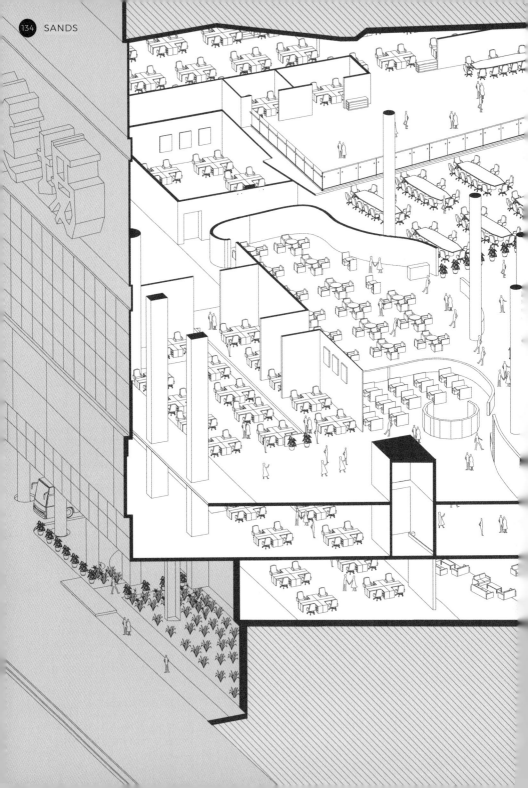

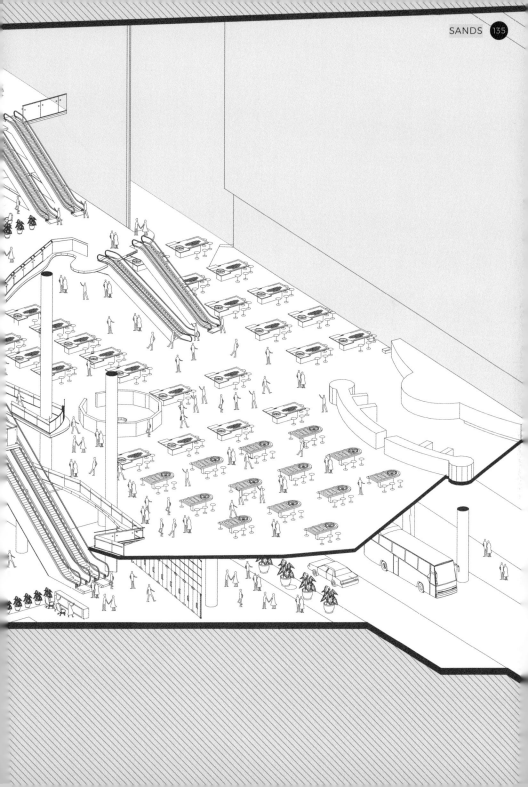

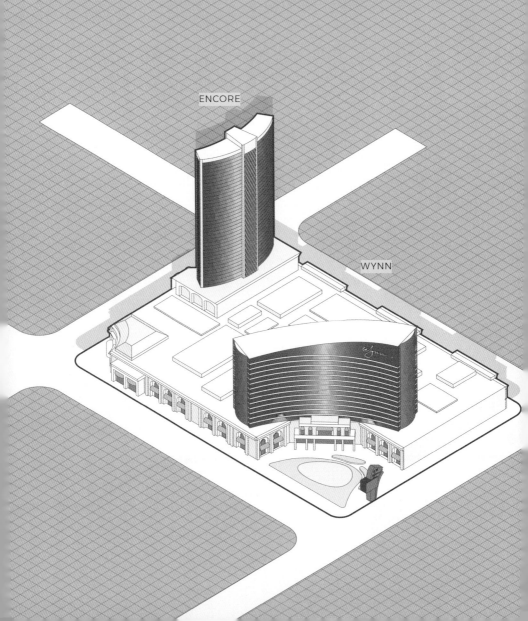

ENCORE

WYNN

B2

WYNN / ENCORE

YEAR OPENED:
2006 / 2010

ROOMS:
1014 (600 / 414)

OPERATOR:
WYNN RESORTS

HEIGHT:
206 m

Casino mogul Steve Wynn built the minimalist, crescent-shaped Wynn and Encore towers, part of the same complex, as smaller copper twins of his identically named Las Vegas resorts. Even though his complex absorbed six entire Macau city blocks, he still lacked space to build a full Las Vegas-sized casino resort.

Nevertheless, Wynn, known for his "wow-factor" attractions, fronted the complex with a musical fountain. He decked the lobby with a golden animatronic dragon that every hour curled out of a carved ceiling engraved with all signs of the zodiac. Meanwhile, designer Roger Thomas introduced to Macau a more sophisticated level of casino design, with lavishly decorated interiors, including cherry-red, glass-blown chandeliers and floral carpets in a predominantly red tone — a color Chinese consider the luckiest.

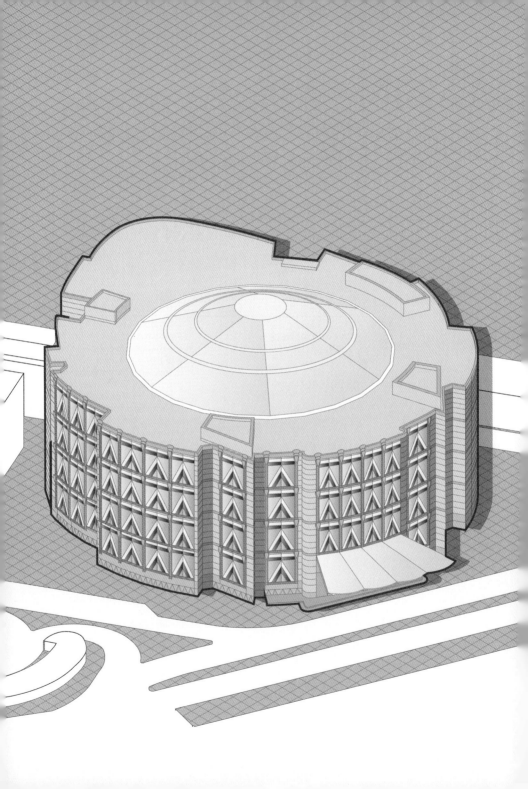

B3

CASINO BABYLON

YEAR OPENED:
2006

ROOMS:
72
(IN THE ROCKS HOTEL)

OPERATOR:
SOCIEDADE DE
JOGOS DE MACAU

HEIGHT:
60 m

Art Deco meets Mesopotamia at Casino Babylon on Fisherman's Wharf, Macau's first theme park with replicas of the Roman Colosseum, Amsterdam canal houses, and a Tang Dynasty palace, next to a fiberglass volcano. The detached casino building is covered in jade-green Art Deco style panels and terracotta walls with Babylonian details. Inside, a sun-shaped chandelier shines within a circle of twelve columns topped by statues of all signs of the zodiac.

The Rocks Hotel is the Babylon's de facto hotel, while neither attached to the casino nor remotely similar in style. The white building with its teal-blue balconies appears an oversized Portuguese colonial mansion.

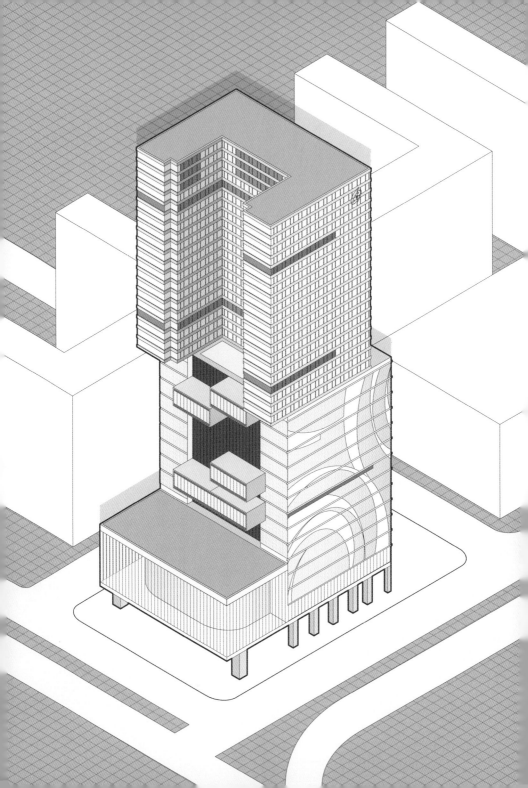

B4

STARWORLD

YEAR OPENED:
2006

ROOMS:
507

OPERATOR:
GALAXY ENTERTAINMENT
GROUP

HEIGHT:
148 m

Hong Kong architect Rocco Yim set the StarWorld apart from existing casinos with a sleeker and more contemporary deconstructivist style. He broke down the scale of the thirty-eight-story building by designing a number of stacked boxes, each individually articulated with different-colored glass and swirls of dot patterns.

But the Star World also broke local building regulations, with a four-story box containing the casino cantilevering right over a public street. An undulating aluminum panel blocks the glass façade from inside, to make sure that gamblers don't know whether it's night or day.

FEMALE ENTRANCE
RECEPTIONIST,
23 YEARS OLD

"I wanted to be a model since
I was small. A year ago, to look
for more opportunities, I left my
hometown in Hunan and came
to Macau to join a modeling
agency. However, after I arrived
to Macau, I realized there were
fewer modeling jobs than
I expected. At the same time,
I discovered that many hotels
hire tall girls as entrance ladies.
Due to a lack of modeling jobs,
I applied here and started
working in the StarWorld
Hotel. They like me very much
because they love hiring tall
girls. Some visitors even ask
to take photos with us, which
makes me very glad. Although
there's still a long way to go to
be a successful model, working
here, and seeing different
visitors brings me some fun!"

B5

MGM GRAND

YEAR OPENED:
2007

ROOMS:
593

OPERATOR:
MGM RESORTS
INTERNATIONAL

HEIGHT:
154 m

MGM Macau's thirty-six-story, deconstructivist-style hotel tower consists of three stacked slabs — colored in silver, gold and rose gold — that each ripple out of sync, suggesting water. Undulating shapes articulate the vast, three-story casino base. Yet without any openings, the complex shuts itself off from the city with a half-mile-long windowless wall.

In contrast to the building's bleak exterior, the interior features a replica of a Portuguese plaza, complete with trees, a fountain, a sinuous black-and-white-tiled floor, a copy of Lisbon's main train station enhanced with a dramatic ceremonial staircase, and "outdoor" dining — all underneath a glass roof. The lobby features the Dalinian Dancer, Salvador Dali's bronze sculpture, dancing underneath Dale Chihuly's glass-blown flowers.

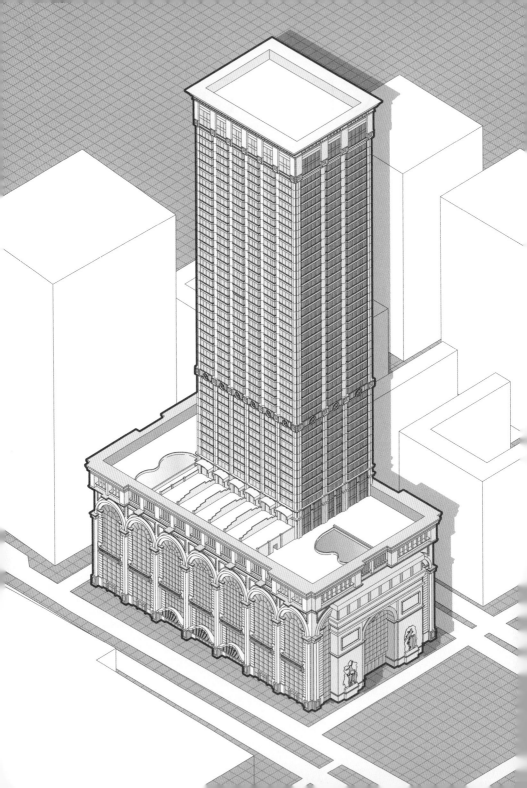

B6

L'ARC

YEAR OPENED:
2009

ROOMS:
301

OPERATOR:
SOCIEDADE DE
JOGOS DE MACAU

HEIGHT:
217 m

L'Arc takes its name and influence from L'Arc de Triomphe — which itself is a Neoclassical version of Roman architecture. Two sandstone copies of the Parisian arch are plastered on the casino's shimmering, gold-plated façades. The buildings' long sides feature a colossal order that evoke a large 1920s bank building, such as the Chicago Fed. The casino base also features fake balconies, statues of stone figures, and bronze, horse-drawn chariots. In contrast, the fifty-three-story hotel tower is only decorated with long, bare columns and a cornice. L'Arc is another "veneered box," a square-shaped casino-hotel built by casino mogul Stanley Ho.

The lobby houses a massive pot of gold, a symbol of good fortune.

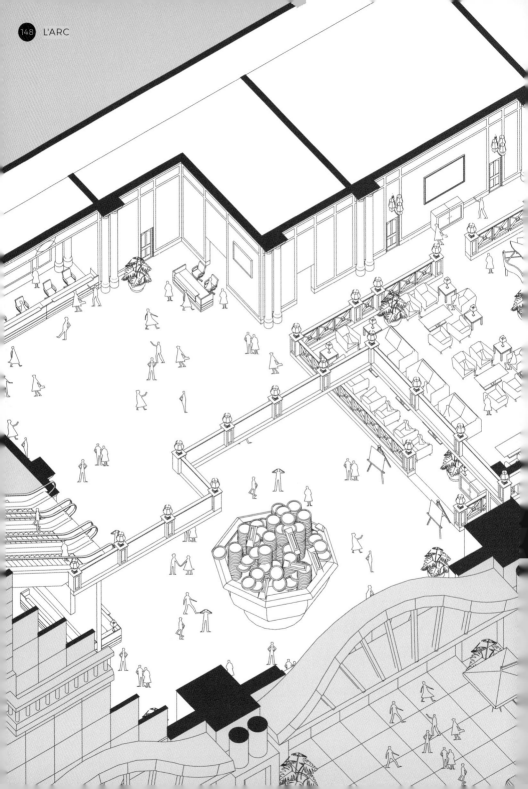

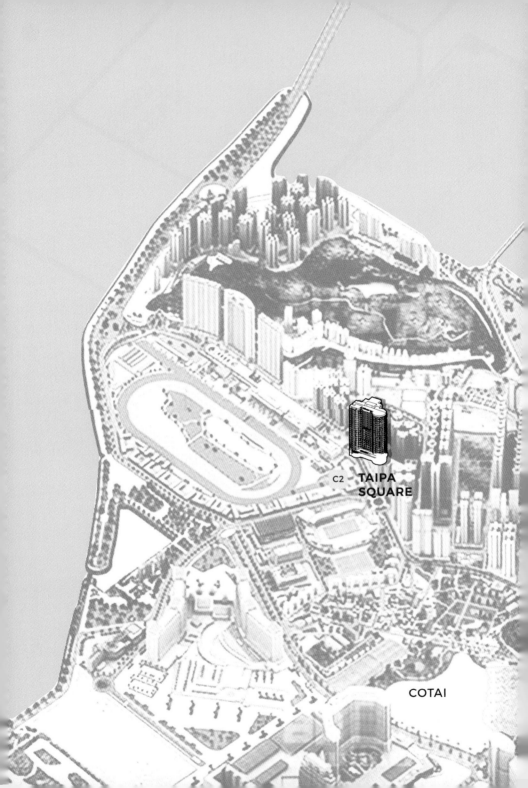

C2 **TAIPA SQUARE**

COTAI

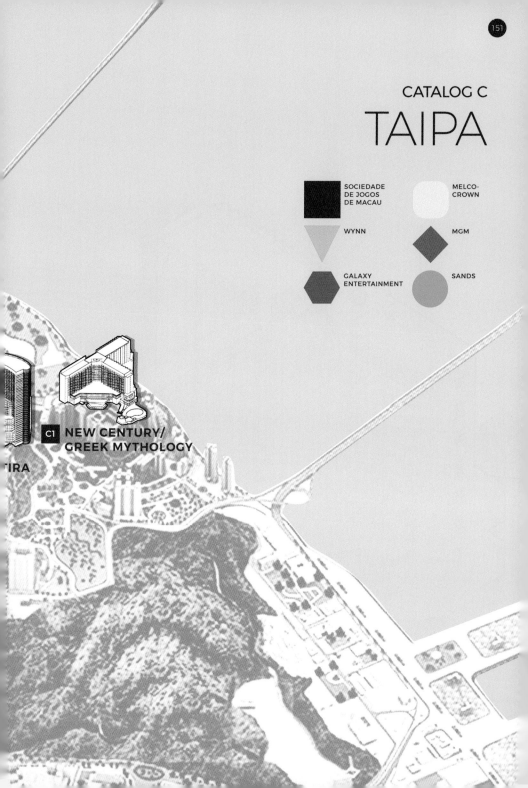

CATALOG C

TAIPA

SOCIEDADE
DE JOGOS
DE MACAU

MELCO-
CROWN

WYNN

MGM

GALAXY
ENTERTAINMENT

SANDS

C1 **NEW CENTURY/
GREEK MYTHOLOGY**

'IRA

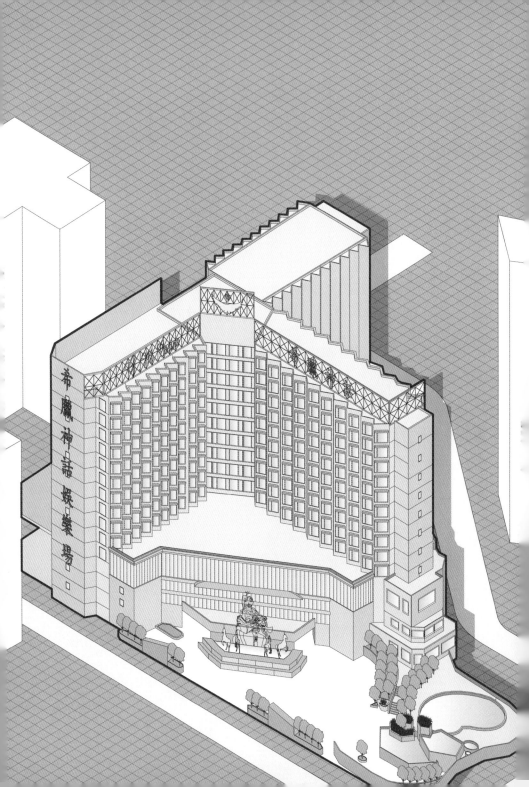

希臘神話娛樂場

C1

NEW CENTURY

YEAR OPENED:
1992

ROOMS:
554

OPERATOR:
SOCIEDADE DE
JOGOS DE MACAU

HEIGHT:
44 m

When it opened in 1992, busloads of Chinese tourists marveled at the New Century's fountain with a plaster figure of Poseidon, trident in hand, surrounded by winged horses and open-mouthed fish. The windows of the modernist hotel were angled to maximize room views, giving the building a faceted expression. The highlight was the lobby with its Roman murals, where a wide marble staircase led visitors past centurion statues and Greek columns to a giant Zeus, sitting on his throne, holding his thunderbolts.

Barely two decades later, the statues and the modern hotel building look faded, and buses pass the New Century for newer and more spectacular casinos.

MALE RESTAURANT CASHIER, 35 YEARS OLD.

"This is my first job since I immigrated to Macau. I have worked here for about nine years. It was splendid at first, but later, new casinos opened, one after the other. They are more modern and luxurious. So we have no edge to our competition. Today, few people come and we make little money.

Most of the customers are from mainland China. Since our staff speaks Chinese instead of English, I think we will lose foreign customers. Hotel management could easily improve things but they just don't care. No concern about us whatsoever. So many of us have lost our passion to work here. I really want to quit and find another job, but this is where I have worked for so long. I miss the better days and friends from the past. I hope the hotel can do something to improve."

C2

TAIPA SQUARE

YEAR OPENED:
2005

ROOMS:
406

OPERATOR:
MELCO-CROWN

HEIGHT:
76 m

Taipa Square opened as a hotel in 2005. Its sandstone-colored tiled and circular-shaped buildings, while not particularly attractive, at least blended into the island's residential neighborhood. But with foreign companies building more profitable casino-hotels, in 2008, Taipa Square decided to retrofit. It installed a luxurious hotel lobby on top and a three-story casino on the ground, decorated with a band of blinding LED lights.

The Chinese-style modernist tower features a row of round windows — seen by some Chinese visitors as "coins," supposed to help the casino collect gamblers' money.

TAIPA SQUARE INTERVIEW:
MALE LOCAL, 40 YEARS OLD

"My home is a ten-minute walk from here. I am a frequent user of this hotel although I have never stayed here. It has the nearest casino to my home, and I always come for gambling only. The casino is not large but it is really convenient for me.

I don't really care about the design and decoration of the hotel, since I am here only for gambling. The first three floors have more than thirty gambling tables. Sometimes, after a few hours of gambling, I will go to the Mocha Café on the second floor. The restaurants on the third floor are good too, and I sometimes come with my family on Sunday morning. Most of the costumers of the restaurants are local citizens who live nearby. I frequently see my neighbor with his family.

Other than the casino and restaurants, I have never been to other floors or even to the main lobby, which is located on the top floor. Therefore, I don't even know if I can recommend the hotel to my friends or not."

C3

ALTIRA

YEAR OPENED:
2007

ROOMS:
218

OPERATOR:
MELCO CROWN

HEIGHT:
160 m

Hong Kong architects Wong Tung & Partners designed the thirty-eight-story Altira, the tallest building on Taipa Island. Instead of another box-shaped casino base, they built a tiered, curvilinear glass façade with an integrated light show that seemed to flow into the glass hotel tower. The rooftop lobby provides panoramic views of the Macau peninsula, thanks to floor-to-ceiling windows. In contrast, pedestrians on the street are presented with a blank west elevation: a fourteen-story windowless wall. As contemporary as the Altira may be, it shuts itself off from the city and fails to contribute to Macau's street life.

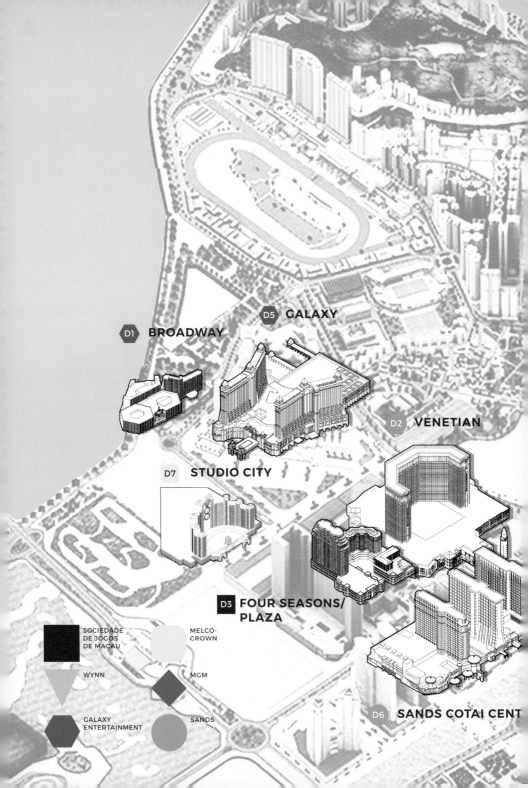

D1 BROADWAY

D5 GALAXY

D2 VENETIAN

D7 STUDIO CITY

D3 FOUR SEASONS/PLAZA

SOCIEDADE DE JOGOS DE MACAU

MELCO-CROWN

WYNN

MGM

GALAXY ENTERTAINMENT

SANDS

D6 SANDS COTAI CENT

CATALOG D
COTAI

TAIPA

D4 **CITY OF DREAMS**

D1

BROADWAY

YEAR OPENED:
2006

ROOMS:
320

OPERATOR:
GALAXY ENTERTAINMENT
GROUP

HEIGHT:
43 m

The Broadway opened in 2006 as the Grand Waldo. While technically the first Cotai casino resort, built on an area large enough to provide a luxury resort experience, it lacked entertainment and refinement. An unimaginative blue, mirror-glass box featured a sign with a flying goddess riding on wavy petals of a golden lotus.

A 2015 remodeling removed the sign, added a 3,000-seat theatre, and connected it to the adjacent Galaxy resort with an elevated bridge across the street. Nevertheless, even in this converted form and with a new name, Broadway, it remains the Galaxy's ugly stepsister.

**MALE CHEF OF THE
HOTEL'S BBQ,
23 YEARS OLD**

"I left my hometown Zhongshan when I was twenty years old and have been a chef in Macau for three years. My uncle worked in the Grand Waldo Hotel, so one day he introduced me to a job here. I am eager to work since the salary for a chef here is better than in China. I didn't know anything about cooking in the beginning, so I started as a dishwasher cleaning the barbeque kitchenware. I am grateful that I had this opportunity to work abroad. Usually, low-skilled people like me, such as my friends who stayed in China, get a very low pay.

However, when I am working and look at the mainland [the hotel has a view of mainland China], I still miss my early days. Hopefully, I can earn enough to move back to my hometown and open a small restaurant."

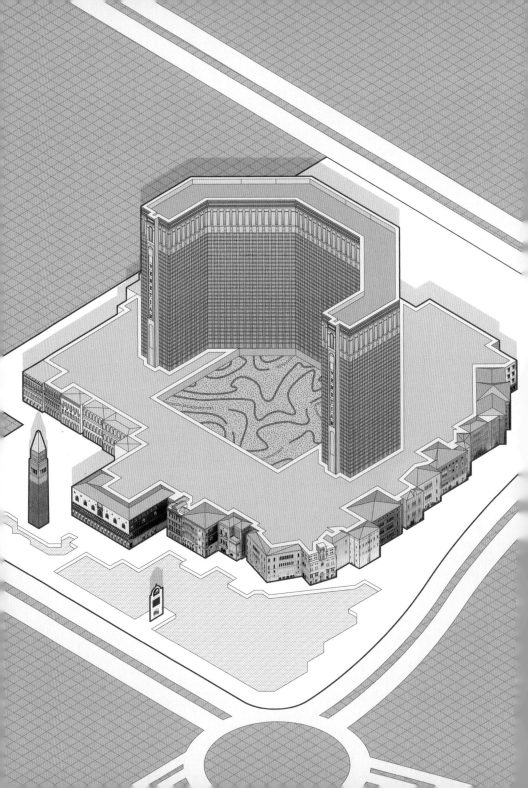

D2

VENETIAN

YEAR OPENED:
2007

ROOMS:
3,000

OPERATOR:
LAS VEGAS SANDS

HEIGHT:
150 m

Casino mogul Sheldon Adelson built the Venetian Macao as a copy of his Venetian Las Vegas, which in turn copies of Venice. He created Cotai's first "must-see" destination, expanding Macau's architectural offerings with Venetian Gothic and Renaissance monuments, including the Campanile, the Doge's Palace, and the St. Mark's Clock Tower. Tapping into retail, a new important revenue stream besides gambling, it includes a luxurious one-million-square-foot indoor mall modeled after the Grand Canal, complete with gondoliers serenading "O Sole Mio."

The Venetian opened in 2007 as Macau's first megaresort, the world's largest casino with 3,400 slot machines, 800 gaming tables, and the planet's seventh largest building by floor area.

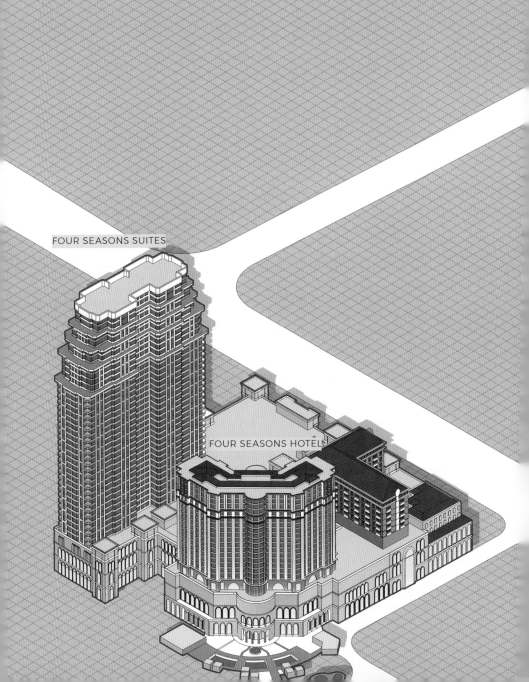

FOUR SEASONS SUITES

FOUR SEASONS HOTEL

D3
PLAZA

YEAR OPENED:
2008

ROOMS:
360

OPERATOR:
SANDS

HEIGHT:
140 m

After casino tycoon Sheldon Adelson built the Venetian to attract hordes of tourists, he expanded the complex with the Plaza casino for wealthier visitors wanting to escape the crowds. He also deviated from the Venetian look, using a pastel-orange façade with arched windows and balconies that evoke colonial Portugal rather than the Italian Renaissance. The entrance to the three-story mall is decorated with Portuguese blue-tinted tiles and lacks a replica canal and Venetian storefronts.

The complex includes nineteen grand invitation-only suites and a thirty-story luxury apartment building, making it possible to reside inside a casino complex.

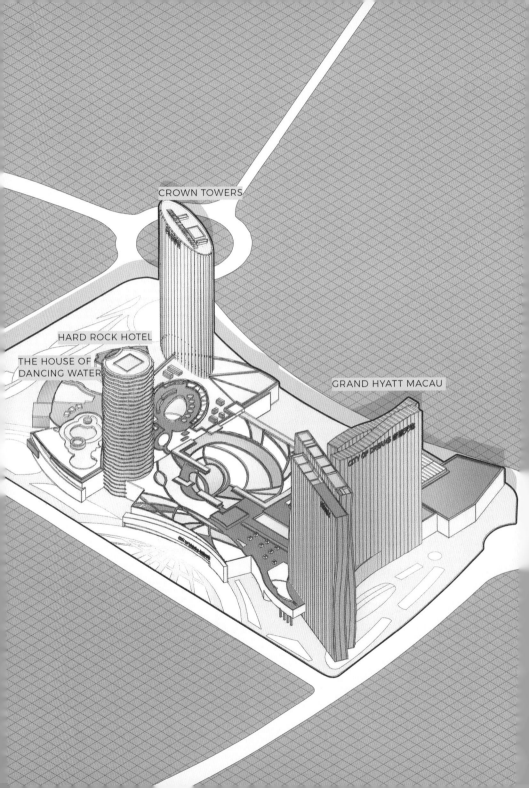

CROWN TOWERS

HARD ROCK HOTEL

THE HOUSE OF
DANCING WATER

GRAND HYATT MACAU

D4

CITY OF DREAMS

YEAR OPENED:
2009

ROOMS:
1,400

OPERATOR:
MELCO CROWN

HEIGHT:
128 m

Built right across from its archrival the Venetian, the City of Dreams competes not with a historic Campanile but with contemporary, curvilinear, glass-finned towers. Instead of a replica Grand Canal, it uses a modern landscape of reflective pools to exploit water for good *feng shui*. As an alternative to idyllic Venetian scenes, it employs a "Vquarium" to draw in the hordes: a sixty-foot-wide video wall teasing tourists with an occasional glimpse of a swimming mermaid.

The complex, designed by American architecture firms The Jerde Partnership and Arquitectonica, encompasses three separate hotel brands: Crown Hotel, Hyatt, and Hard Rock. In 2017, it will expand with an even more contemporary, organically shaped tower that features a soaring, 40-meter-high atrium, designed by the star architect Zaha Hadid.

MALE VISITOR,
25 YEARS OLD

"I came here from mainland China for tourism. The City of Dreams is the third casino I have visited so far. I just saw the Venetian casino this afternoon. The City of Dreams is more contemporary than other casinos.

My favorite is the mermaid in the lobby. First, I really thought it was an actual person floating in the water. Later I found it was a 3D-holographic image. We also have this technology in the mainland, but it is not as creatively used.

I bought a silk scarf for my girlfriend in the shops at the boulevard. Walking along this boulevard you can go round the entire City of Dreams. Some doors lead to the casino, located in the center. But today I don't want to go to the casino; I just want to experience the ambience.

The three hotel lobbies here are very different. My favorite is the lobby of the Hard Rock Hotel. To my surprise, there are clothes and gloves of Michael Jackson and Madonna on display, as well as items from Elvis Presley, Jacky Cheung, and other pop stars. I have taken a lot of pictures.

I am sorry. I must rush off now. I hope to visit the Sands Hotel today."

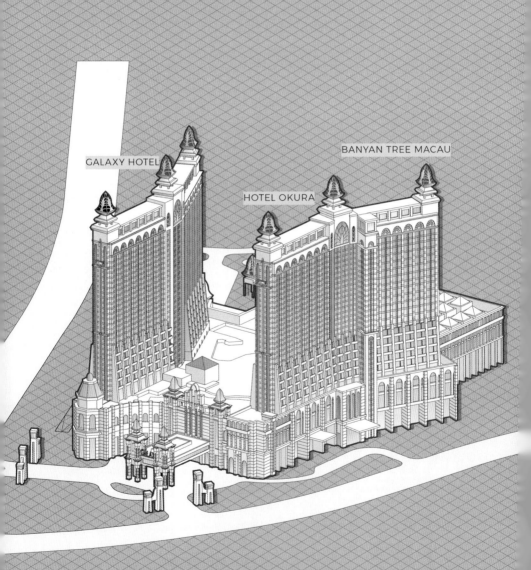

GALAXY HOTEL

BANYAN TREE MACAU

HOTEL OKURA

D5

GALAXY

YEAR OPENED:
2011

ROOMS:
3,600

OWNER:
GALAXY ENTERTAINMENT
GROUP

HEIGHT:
148 m

In contrast to other Cotai resorts that derive their looks from historic European or contemporary architectural themes, the Galaxy set itself apart with a Southeast Asian touch. Theme-park designer Gary Goddard designed the Galaxy as "must-see" Buddhist castle, complete with 24-carat-gold-plated windows and Mughal-style, bulbous cupolas shooting laser beams, visible across Macau. The complex consists of three Asian hotel brands: Banyan Tree, Hotel Okura, and the Galaxy Hotel. A white sand beach with tropical gardens, a wave pool, and a 575-foot-long river ride — Macau's largest pool — attracts tourists as well as locals.

Symbols of prosperity lure guests at the two entrances. The main lobby captivates visitors with a fountain that floats a massive, color-changing diamond below a circular dome decorated with patterns of peacock feathers. The bus entrance features a shimmering, foggy pool with flickering multicolored crystals.

**LOCAL FEMALE RESIDENT,
27 YEARS OLD**

"Galaxy has made a significant
impact on the community
of Macau, particularly to my
generation. Besides bringing
us a lot of job opportunities, I
would say its most influential
impact was bringing the UA
cinema to Macau. Before, there
were no 3D-films at all. We had
no IMAX, no 3D Avatar. We, the
young generation, had to make
trips to Hong Kong to see such
movies, which is very costly.

Today, the UA cinema in Macau
has the largest selection of films.
There is even a director's club
where you can privately book the
entire theatre all to yourselves
to watch films with your own
group of friends! The food court
provides a wide selection of
cuisines from all over the world.
It is slightly overpriced but still
reasonable. The artificial beach is
also a highlight, though us locals
don't have much opportunity
to use it. I particularly like Hotel
Okura since all the female
staff in the lobby are dressed
in kimonos and they politely
curtsy to every passerby."

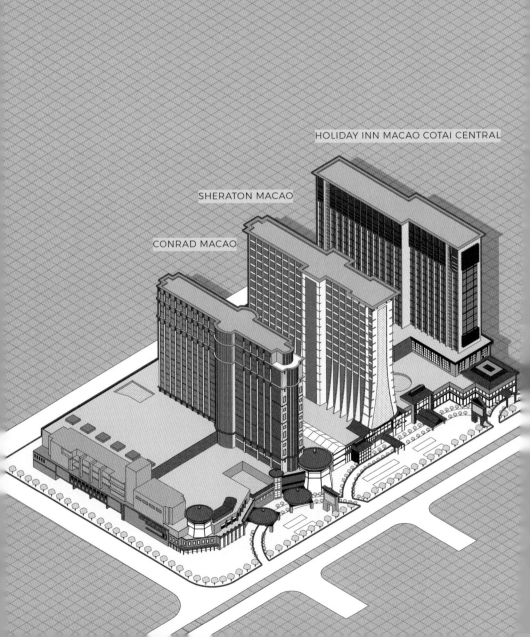

HOLIDAY INN MACAO COTAI CENTRAL

SHERATON MACAO

CONRAD MACAO

D6

SANDS COTAI CENTRAL

YEAR OPENED:
2012

ROOMS:
6,000

OWNER:
LAS VEGAS SANDS

HEIGHT:
125 m

In contrast to his European-themed Venetian casino, American business tycoon Sheldon Adelson deliberately built his Sands Cotai Central with Asian sensibilities. Tibetan-style buildings and pagoda-roofs decorate the vast casino base. Three massive, modern hotel towers are detailed to suggest timber-frames and roofs. Inside, a statue of Caishen, the bearded, Chinese god of prosperity, overlooks an idyllic botanic garden and a spraying fountain underneath a glass-roof. Rocks, palm trees, and waterfalls lend a Polynesian look to the shopping mall, complete with timed, tropical rain showers.

The complex includes Conrad, Sheraton, and Holiday Inn hotel, giving the Sands Cotai Central a total of 6,000 rooms — the world's third largest hotel.

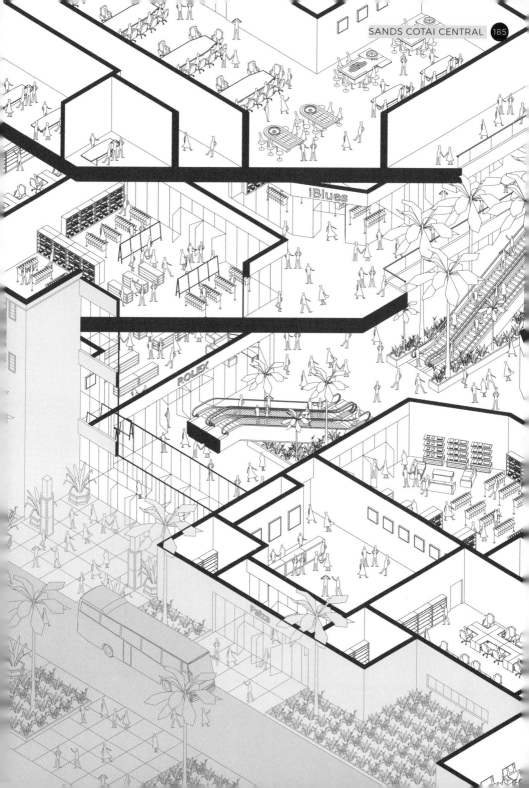

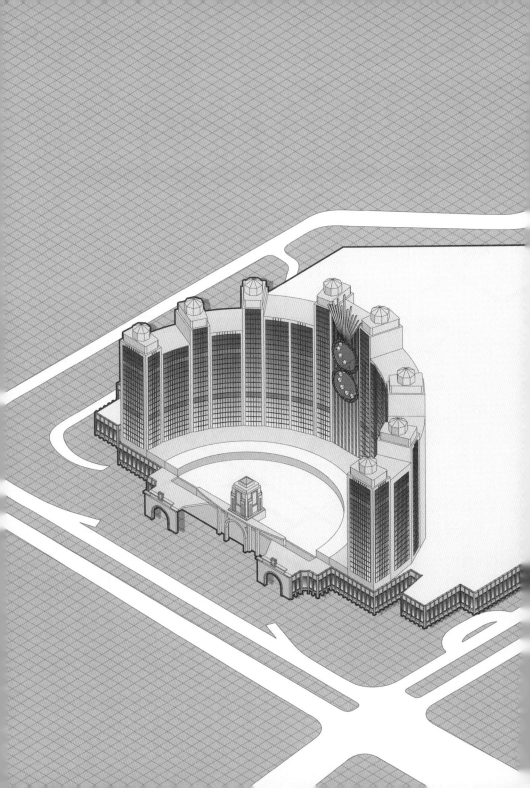

D7

STUDIO CITY

YEAR OPENED:
2015

ROOMS:
1,600

OWNER:
MELCO-CROWN

HEIGHT:
152 m

The $3.2 billion Studio City is a tribute to both Hollywood and Disney's Enchanted Castle and emblematic of Macau's attempt to diversity gambling with entertainment. Gary Goddard, a former Disney theme-park designer, designed the building after Batman's Gotham City, mixing Art Deco and German Expressionism. He perforated the thirty-five-story structure with two bright holes, as if two asteroids had shot through the building. It features a 430-foot-tall attraction: the world's first Ferris wheel shaped in a figure eight, a number that Chinese consider the luckiest.

Two thirty-foot "Heroes of Steel" statues greet visitors at the entrance. Inside, guests can ride Wonder Woman go-karts, a Batman virtual reality simulation, and watch a specially-commissioned fifteen-minute film by Martin Scorcese, featuring Leonardo DiCaprio and Robert De Niro, inside the resort's television and film production facilities. But the best attraction is the Golden Reel Ferris wheel with panoramic views over the Cotai Strip: only two decades ago a swampland, and today the world's highest grossing casino conglomeration.

COMPARING CASINO MOTIFS

SIGNS OF SPILLING RICHES

RIO

GRAND EMPEROR

PRESIDENT

LOTUS SHAPES

LISBOA

GRAND LISBOA

WYNN

CONTEMPORARY ARCHITECTURE

NEOHISTORIC ARCHITECTURE

MGM GRAND

VENETIAN

STARWORLD

GALAXY

ALTIRA

L' ARC

COMPARING CASINO ELEVATORS

RIO   LISBOA   FOUR SEASONS

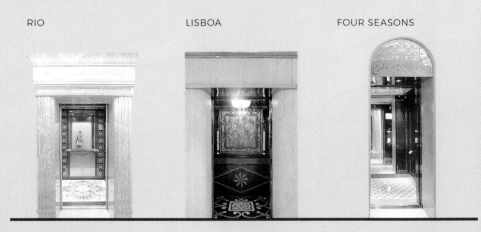

DOORFRAMES

L'ARC   STARWORLD   TAIPA SQUARE

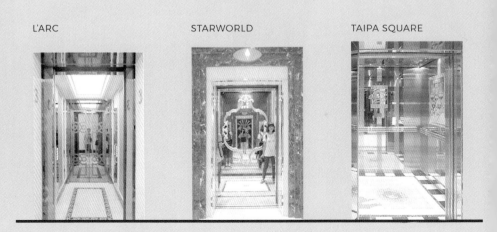

FULL-LENGTH MIRRORS

WYNN ALTIRA MGM GRAND

HALF-MIRRORS

VENETIAN GALAXY GRAND LISBOA

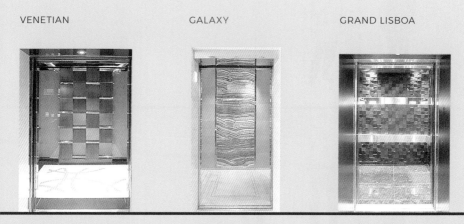

CERAMIC TILE WALLS

COMPARING CASINO OUTFITS

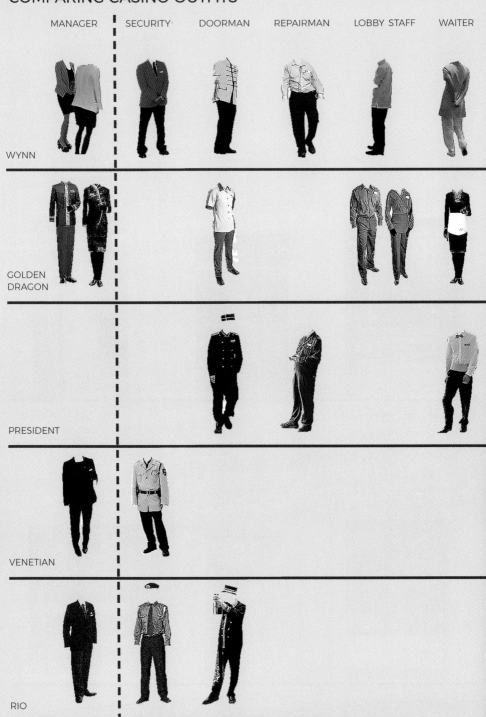

	MANAGER	SECURITY	DOORMAN	REPAIRMAN	LOBBY STAFF	WAITER
WYNN						
GOLDEN DRAGON						
PRESIDENT						
VENETIAN						
RIO						

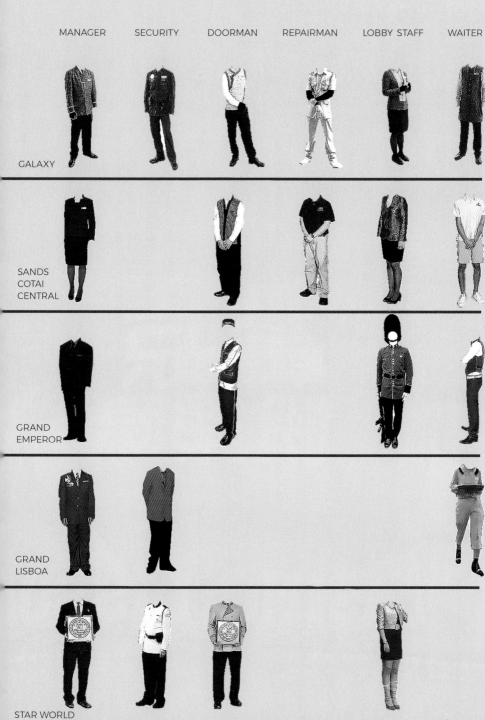

CASINO LISBOA

RIO

L'ARC

ALTIRA

SANDS

VENETIAN

VENETIAN

MGM GRAND

GALAXY

CASINO LISBOA

Photo: Adam Nowek

VENETIAN

WYNN

GRAND EMPEROR

VENETIAN

VENETIAN

Welcome to
The Venetian

欢迎光

澳门威尼

COTAI CENTRAL

注意 WARNING
扶手电梯级两亲的缝隙中干
Keep footwear away from
edges of escalator

CONTRIBUTORS

Cathryn H. Clayton is a cultural anthropologist and Associate Professor in the Asian Studies Program at the University of Hawaii, Mānoa. Her first book, *Sovereignty at the Edge: Macau and the Question of Chineseness* (2009), won the 2010 Francis L. K. Hsu Award for best new book on East Asia from the Society for East Asian Anthropology in the American Anthropological Association. She has a forthcoming monograph about the Cultural Revolution-style protests in Macau in 1966 that nearly toppled the Portuguese colonial administration. She has studied at Williams College, Stanford University, and the University of California, Santa Cruz, and held an An Wang Postdoctoral Fellowship at Harvard University's Fairbank Center. She taught at the University of Macau from 2001–2005.

Thomas Daniell is currently Head of the Department of Architecture at the University of Saint Joseph, Macau, and Visiting Professor at the University of Hong Kong and University of Tokyo. He holds a BArch with honors from Victoria University of Wellington, an MEng from Kyoto University, and a PhD from RMIT University, Melbourne. Widely published, his books include *FOBA: Buildings* (2005), *After the Crash: Architecture in Post-Bubble Japan* (2008), *Houses and Gardens of Kyoto* (2010), *Kiyoshi Sey Takeyama + Amorphe* (2011), *Kansai 6* (2011), and *An Anatomy of Influence* (2017).

Miao He is a PhD candidate in Department of Business Administration at the University of Macau. She teaches in the Department of International Trade and Finance, Zhuhai College of Jilin University. Her research on casino gaming policy has appeared in publications such as the *Journal of Gambling Business and Economics*. She also focuses on regional economics, especially Macau and the Pearl River Delta, with articles published in books including *The New Macao SAR* (in Chinese, 2011) and *China's Macao Transformed: Challenge and Development in the 21st Century* (2014).

HK Urbex (Hong Kong Urban Exploration) is an anonymous, grassroots collective that seeks to unearth and document hidden sites in and around Hong Kong. Beyond the shimmering skyscrapers and glitzy malls, the intrepid explorers reveal another side of Hong Kong and the Asian cities they visit, immortalizing and bringing undisclosed nonspaces to light (www.hkurbex.com).

Desmond Lam is Associate Professor of International Integrated Resort Management, University of Macau, and a life member of Clare Hall (University of Cambridge). He has been one of the judges for the International Gaming Awards (London) since 2008 and an academic affairs advisor to the Macau Gaming Management Association since 2012. Desmond has written and presented extensively on gaming-related issues, and his articles are featured in premier trade and academic publications. He is author of the book *Chopsticks and Gambling* (2014), which examines the little-known world of Chinese gambling from historical, cultural, psychological, and social perspectives. Over the years, Desmond has received several research and industry awards, including the 2015 Cambridge Clare Hall Fellowship and the Emerging Leader trophy at the 2016 Asia Gaming Awards. He has conducted numerous university courses and executive workshops in gaming, tourism, and hospitality.

Kah-Wee Lee is Assistant Professor at the Department of Architecture, National University of Singapore. He worked as a planner in the Urban Redevelopment Authority before joining academia. Currently, he teaches history and theory of urban planning in the Masters of Urban Planning program. Kah-Wee's research bridges the contemporary migration of the casino industry from Las Vegas to Macau and Singapore and the history of the control of vice in Southeast Asia. He has published in *Geoforum*, the *International Journal of Urban and Regional Research* and *Environment and Planning A and C*, and is working on a book about casino urbanism. Kah-Wee is a member of the Tan Kah Kee International Society and volunteers in events related to youth and education.

Adam Nowek is an urban researcher, architectural photographer, and Managing Editor at The Proto City. His primary areas of research are pop-up city making, high-rise residential architecture, and Vancouverism. He edited *Pop-Up City: City-Making in a Fluid World* (2014). His photography focuses on comparative studies of architectural typologies and urban spaces in transition. Adam has contributed photography to three book-length projects by Stefan Al, including *Mall City: Hong Kong's Dreamworlds of Consumption* (2016) and *The Strip: Las Vegas and the Architecture of the American Dream* (2017).

Tim Simpson is Associate Dean of the Faculty of Social Sciences, and Associate Professor of Communication at the University of Macau, where he has worked since 2001. He is the coauthor (with UK-based photographer Roger Palmer) of *Macao Macau* (2015) and editor of *Tourist Utopias: Offshore Islands, Enclave Spaces, and Mobile Imaginaries* (2017), as well as authoring a variety of academic articles and essays about Macau's postcolonial development.

Ricardo C. S. Siu is Associate Professor of Business Economics at the University of Macau. He served as program coordinator of Economics and International Finance (2001–2004) and Gaming Management (2005–2009), as well as the Acting Head of the Department of Finance and Business Economics (2011–2012) at the Faculty of Business Administration. He is an internationally known scholar in the stream of casino gaming, specializing in public policy and the evolution of casino gaming in Macao and other Asian jurisdictions. He has many publications in academic journals, professional magazines, and books, including the *Journal of Economic Issues, Journal of Gambling Studies, International Gaming Studies, Journal of Gambling Business and Economics, UNLV Gaming Research and Review Journal,* and *Gaming Law Reviews and Economics.* His article "The Economics of Asian Casino Gaming and Gambling" is published in *The Oxford Handbook of the Economics of Gambling* (2013).

ABOUT THE EDITOR

Stefan Al is an architect, urban designer, scholar, educator, and author, currently serving as Associate Professor of Urban Design at the University of Pennsylvania.

He is acclaimed for his work on Asian urbanism, with books investigating China's informal settlements and Hong Kong's compact urban form, including *Factory Towns of South China: An Illustrated Guidebook* (2012); *Villages in the City: A Guide to South China's Informal Settlements* (2014); *Mall City: Hong Kong's Dreamworlds of Consumption* (2016); and *Macau and the Casino Complex.* He has made significant contributions to understanding the role of branding in cities, highlighted in his most recent book, *The Strip: Las Vegas and the Architecture of the American Dream* (2017).

Al's career as a practicing architect includes work on renowned projects such as the 2,000-feet-high Canton Tower in Guangzhou. He has also served as an advisor to the Hong Kong government, consulting on the development of the city's harbor and external lighting guidelines; the Chinese government, advising on new urban design guidelines; and the United Nations High-Level Political Forum on Sustainable Development.

CREDITS

Layout Design and Graphic Editing
Anthony Lam and Ramune Bartuskaite

Infographics
Global Gaming Revenue 2001-2014: Yizhou Feng
Urban Morphology 1557-2016: Mei Yan Cheung
Macau Land Reclamation 1912-2011: Kevin Yunke
Qu, Ying Yin, Melissa Yuen Shan Liu
Free Spectacle Map: Alice Weng Sam Iu
Casino Revenue Composition: Jun Chen
Casinos in Macau: Yizhou Feng, Lansheng Chen,
Jia Peng, Kai On Teng
Casino Motifs, Casino Elevators, Casino Outfits,
Casino Facades: Sarah Xiaoyun Xu, Mia Xiangmei
Hong, Minqiao Du
Casino Heights: Jun Chen, Yihua Shen, Mahtab
Hussain Siddique, Howard Ho Chung Au

Drawings
Casino Lisboa: Jia Peng
President: Cici Ziqiong Yang
Grand Lapa: Rahul Muni Bajracharya
Holiday Inn: Kalpesh Dilip Narkhede
Golden Dragon: Aqua Yuting Ouyang
Casa Real: Sylvia Si Cai
Grand Emperor: Yizhe Zhang
Rio: Kevin Yunke Qu
Grand Lisboa: Alice Weng Sam Iu
Ponte 16: Zhenzhen Chen
Sands: Mahtab Hussain Siddique
Wynn / Encore: Mia Xiangmei Hong
Casino Babylon: Kai On Teng
Starworld: Morning Muling Jiang
MGM Grand: Mei Yan Cheung
L'Arc: Sarah Xiaoyun Xu
New Century: Wei Xue
Taipa Square: Melissa Yuen Shan Liu
Altira: Ying Yin
Broadway: Howard Ho Chung Au
Venetian: Minqiao Du
Plaza: Yihua Shen
City of Dreams: Lansheng Chen
Galaxy: Yizhou Feng
Sands Cotai Central: Jun Chen
Studio City: David Zhewei Feng

Interviews
Grand Lisboa: Alice Weng Sam Iu
Starworld: Morning Muling Jiang
New Century: Wei Xue
Taipa Square: Melissa Yuen Shan Liu
Broadway: Howard Ho Chung Au
City of Dreams: Lansheng Chen
Galaxy: Yizhou Feng

Case Study Text
Stefan Al

Photos by Adam Nowek
Starworld, City of Dreams, Galaxy, Wynn,
Venetian, Cotai

INDEX